LIBRARY TRAINING GUIDES

Training library assistants

Margaret Lobban

Library Association Publishing

© Library Association Publishing 1997

Library Association Publishing is wholly owned by The Library Association

Published by
Library Association Publishing
7 Ridgmount Street
London WC1E 7AE

First published 1997

British Library Cataloguing in Publication Data.
A catalogue record for this book is available from the British Library.

ISBN 1-85604-139-5

Typeset in 11/12pt Palermo from author's disk by Library Association Publishing
Printed and made in Great Britain by Amber (Printwork) Ltd, Harpenden, Herts.

Introduction by the Series Editor

This new series of Library Training Guides (LTGs for short) aims to fill the gap left by the demise of the old Training Guidelines published in the 1980s in the wake of The Library Association's work on staff training. The new LTGs develop the original concept of concisely written summaries of the best principles and practice in specific areas of training by experts in the field which give library and information workers a good-quality guide to best practice. Like the original guidelines, the LTGs also include appropriate examples from a variety of library systems as well as further reading and useful contacts.

Though each guide stands in its own right, LTGs form a coherent whole. Acquisition of all LTGs as they are published will result in a comprehensive manual of training and staff development in library and information work.

The guides are aimed at practising librarians and library training officers. They are intended to be comprehensive without being over-detailed; they should give both the novice and the experienced librarian/training officer an overview of what should/could be done in a given situation and in relation to a particular skill/group of library staff/type of library.

David Baker

LIBRARY TRAINING GUIDES

Series Editor: David Baker
Editorial Assistant: Joan Welsby

Other Library Training Guides available

Training needs analysis
Michael Williamson
1-85604-077-1

Induction
Julie Parry
1-85604-078-X

Evaluation
Steve Phillips
1-85604-079-8

Training and development for women
Beryl Morris
1-85604-080-1

Interpersonal skills
Philippa Levy
1-85604-081-X

Management of training and staff development
June Whetherly
1-85604-104-2

Mentoring
Biddy Fisher
1-85604-105-0

Recruitment
Julie Parry
1-85604-106-9

Supporting adult learners
Tony Bamber *et al.*
1-85604-125-5

Presenting information
Clare Nankivell and Michael Shoolbred
1-85604-138-7

Personal professional development and the solo librarian
Sue Lacey Bryant
1-85604-141-7

Team management
Robert Bluck
1-85604-167-0

Contents

Introduction

Overview

The aim of this Library Training Guide is to complement the others in the series by highlighting the specific issues that affect the training of library assistants. It will do this by considering the work in which library assistants are involved and the major influences affecting their jobs and training, focusing primarily on user services in public and academic libraries. Much of the content of this volume may also be applicable to work in special libraries but certain more specialist tasks, such as preparing stock for easy retrieval, indexing, interlibrary loans and literature searching[1] will have higher priority. For further consideration of the training issues specifically posed by special libraries, reference should be made to Sue Lacey Bryant, *Personal professional development and the solo librarian* in this series.[2]

The guide considers different approaches to staff development and the impact that Scottish/National Vocational Qualifications (S/NVQs) will have on the development of training, education and accredited qualifications in the UK. The context will be the development of library assistants' work as a career in its own right.

Finally consideration will be given to managing training in order to ensure its effectiveness for both employee and employer. The issues discussed in the guide are illustrated by bringing together examples of current good practice.

Quality service provision

The guide considers the range of training to which library assistants should have access if their performance is to make a major contribution to the provision of quality services. It aims to develop a motivated, informed member of staff. Four aspects are considered:

- Skills ('how to do the job'). Perhaps the most obvious training offered to library assistants. To be effective, attention must be given to the training needs, the techniques employed and the presentation of the training.
- Attitudes: ensuring staff have effective interpersonal and personal skills to achieve the service objectives. This focuses primarily on the induction process and the importance of all staff incorporating the 'customer care' ethic into their daily work.
- Continuing self development: the aspect of training most frequently overlooked. It concerns staff learning about the organization, and their role within and contribution to it. For this to be achieved, a 'learning environment' must be created that will support training and enhance its effectiveness.

- How the organization and its staff relate to the profession: issues affecting the relationship between training and education will be discussed.

Historical factors

Before the onset of the graduate profession, staff joined a library service and worked their way from junior assistant to fully qualified librarian, taking professional exams *en route*. For that reason there were always sufficient staff at various stages of training and education to render a specific internal training programme for library assistants unnecessary. Following the introduction of graduate status for librarians, library assistants fared badly. Authorities took a long time to acknowledge their responsibilities in providing for the training needs of this group.

The emergence in the UK of the City and Guilds 737 Library Assistants' Certificate marked the start of an educative process and, although it guaranteed advancement neither in post nor in further education, the popularity of the course was evidence of the high motivation and commitment amongst this group of staff. Later, the development of the BTEC National Certificate course and, in Scotland, the National Certificate (and later the Higher National Certificate) gave staff an additional route to follow, albeit still with no guarantee of promotion.

Even now, it is tempting to assume that any training given will facilitate the member of staff becoming professionally qualified. This is indicative of a lack of career structure rather than a comment on the need to be qualified. Increasingly libraries are recognizing the value of well-trained, experienced library assistants in the provision of library services and are doing more to facilitate the creation of a career path suited to their skills.

Training in what?

Throughout the lengthy and often frustrating discussions about training and education for library assistants there has been controversy concerning what should be included: debate has centred on whether the level of work entailed sufficient integrity to allow it to stand on its own. Was an appreciation of the skills of librarianship sufficient to comprise education or was it training? In the early days of the City and Guilds and BTEC courses, one school of thought held that the wide-ranging nature of library work required library assistants to enhance their general knowledge by undertaking a course of liberal or related studies. In some instances this proved a valuable adjunct; in many others it was perceived as a time-filler unworthy of the hours devoted to it. This may reflect the quality of teaching at the time, or it may indicate a narrowness of vision on the part of the trainees. Overall, it suggested that students wanted to be trained to do their job better – to have more understanding of libraries and their own work.

It must be recognized that the content of the library assistant's job involves sufficient variety and complexity to warrant specialist training. Experience of teaching on a variety of different courses indicates that most students want training, not education. Not until the training is sufficiently well understood will the need for education be acknowledged by library assistants. Today there is more of an acceptance that the two can coexist but for them to thrive the environment must be conducive to learning and recognition must be given for skills gained.

References

1   Pantry, S., *The special librarian's view. Library staff training: the problem of non-professional staff training. The proceedings of a symposium held 30th November 1976 at Leeds Polytechnic*, edited by D E Davison, Leeds, Polytechnic School of Librarianship, 1977.

2   Bryant, S. L., *Personal professional development and the solo librarian*, London, Library Association Publishing, 1995.

Library assistant duties and external influences

1.1 Library assistant duties

For many users the library assistant at the counter is 'the library'. It is unimportant whether the person serving them has a degree or a professional qualification as long as the service provided is courteous, knowledgeable, and efficient. The range of work in which library assistants have traditionally been involved varies more in level of work than type or range of work:[1] they are unlikely to be involved in making policy but rather in carrying it out. A well trained workforce of library assistants will support the managerial role of the professionally qualified librarian.

Library assistant duties normally encompass:

- dealing with users, some of whom may have special needs
- circulation duties
- shelving and maintaining the good order of the library
- processing stock
- simple enquiry work
- cataloguing
- children's activity sessions
- working with electronic sources.

The balance of work will be dependent upon the type and size of library but some libraries are now identifying less skilled posts involving primarily shelving or processing.

In the main, library assistants regard the job as a career and recent changes in staff structures are securing posts of considerable responsibility within defined decision boundaries for library assistants. In addition to variety in their work, library assistants need to have a knowledge of the overall context in order to carry out their duties effectively.

1.2 Major influences

- Information technology: computers have been a major influence in all types of libraries. They are now impacting directly on information provision. End-users can access databases through CD-ROM services and therefore expect staff on duty, irrespective of grade, to be able to offer assistance: staff at all levels therefore need to be computer literate. This enhanced skills base has gone hand-in-hand with other influences, which have resulted in library management making better use of their skilled staff.
- Reorganization: many local authorities categorize libraries within a wider recreational remit and in some places this has affected the balance of service provision. A crucial factor is the organizational change

which is prevalent. This may be brought about through local authority boundary changes, convergence of existing departments or merely departmental reorganization to make better use of existing resources. Any of these changes can bring about doubts over job security, which have an adverse effect on staff motivation and performance.

- Charters, service agreements and other quality issues: the 1990s have emphasized customer care, customer rights and quality issues. The widespread introduction of charters and programmes such as Investors in People have emphasized the need for well-trained staff equipped for service provision.
- Self development: these external influences have been concurrent with a shift towards a culture of continuing personal development. This has encouraged able library assistants, possibly unable to follow a full-time course, to pursue qualifications and promotion.

In short, libraries now need a workforce which is flexible and highly skilled. All library staff must learn to cope with working within a changing organization.

1.3 Academic libraries

Major changes in education have taken place in recent years: an emphasis on lifelong learning; the expansion and widening of the student base; the changes in teaching and learning; the increased emphasis on information technology both as a delivery mechanism and a supporting tool.

Within further education, the move to incorporation has made institutions responsible for their own budgets and therefore more responsive to market forces. The increase in franchised courses has caused the traditional levels of tertiary education to become blurred. Libraries are expected to deliver a wider range of services to a greater variety of users without any significant increase in resourcing.

Many of these changes, as they affected Higher Education, are highlighted by the Follett Report[2] which summarizes the major influences as being:

- changes within teaching and learning
- new technology and information systems
- emphasis on customer service
- working in teams.

The Fielden Report[3] focuses on the human resource issues arising from the Follett Report. It highlights the importance of training policies being included in the library's strategic plan. It states that for changes to be taken on board by libraries, staff must be fully developed to enable long term benefits to be offered to the service and the users. The Report identifies a category of 'upskilled' library assistants who will increasingly work with databases and the Internet and who will communicate with teaching staff regularly as part of their normal duties. These staff will use their skills to find technical solutions to the users' information requirements.

This suggested that two types of training will assume a higher priority: technical skills, such as database handling and computing, and personal skills such as communication and team working.[4]

1.4 **Public libraries**

Reorganization within authorities has established area teams under the leadership of an area librarian. This has resulted in branch libraries being run on a day-to-day basis by a senior library assistant, with planning being done at area level. These changes usually result in library assistants having the opportunity to become involved in a wider range of duties than previously, and the expectation that they will assume additional responsibilities.

The recent local authority changes in Scotland, and the forthcoming changes in England and Wales, are also exerting major influences on the working life of library assistants. Concerns about the security of posts is becoming a feature of working life. This can act as a strong de-motivator and requires careful and skilled management. Another strong external pressure is the increased workload resulting from the need to improve productivity. Coping with increased use with very few additional resources can be a detrimental influence if not approached and managed creatively. Sensitively approached, it can give staff at all levels the opportunity to examine their approach to work and to devise more effective ways of carrying out a similar range of duties. For this to be acceptable at library assistant level, the staff must be well informed and have a thorough understanding of their work and those around them.

Much of the external pressure to maintain service levels has resulted from the introduction of charters and service agreements, which require the library service to maintain publicly stated levels irrespective of other influences. Their creation has also made users more aware of their rights and therefore the potential for 'frank discussions' across the counter has increased. Staff skilled in interpersonal skills and library policy are required.

Many public service staff now have increasing concerns about their personal safety and a disconcerting number of libraries are reporting incidents of violence or aggression. For this reason, many libraries now partake in aggression handling training sessions offered by local authorities and The Library Association.

As in academic libraries, information technology is having major impact. Staff at all levels are now expected to be aware and knowledgeable about housekeeping systems, CD-ROMs, Internet and electronic mail. This trend seems set to continue and staff must be prepared constantly to update their skills. But it is not just within the area of IT that variety exists; the range of other formats and services routinely being offered by libraries, such as CDs, videos, and open learning materials, means that library staff need to have a far wider working knowledge of materials than previously. The essential skills now required of a library assistant are the ability to cope with change, IT and interpersonal relationships.

References

1 Baker, D., *Training library assistants*, London, Library Association Publishing, 1986.
2 Joint Funding Councils' Libraries Review Group, *Report (The Follett Report)*, Bristol, HEFCE, 1993.
3 John Fielden Consultancy, *Supporting expansion: a report on human resource management in academic libraries, for the Joint Funding Councils' Libraries Review Group*, Bristol, HEFCE, 1993.

4   Sykes, P., 'Staff development for library assistants', in Oldroyd, M. (ed.), *Staff development in academic libraries: present practice and future challenges*, London, Library Association Publishing, 1996.

2 Content

2.1 Induction

Arriving at a new place of work is probably one of the most memorable and, at the same time, terrifying aspects of work, and therefore it is essential that the induction process is well planned and implemented. Induction presents the organization to the library assistant and therefore can 'speak volumes' about the library's approach to work, staff relations and training. This period is formative. When induction is done well it leaves the member of staff feeling motivated and convinced that s/he has made the right decision in joining the staff. If done badly, it will put the staff member in a doubting frame of mind, which can even lead to the 'motivation crisis' where new staff leave within the first few weeks.

The induction programme serves two primary functions:

- to introduce the organization and the working environment
- to offer a well structured introduction to duties and tasks.

It is probably correct to assume that induction will last for at least six months, the most intensive period being during the first few weeks. However, the exact length of the induction phase is difficult to gauge because it will vary depending upon experience of the staff member and the size of the organization. Irrespective of both these factors, though, it is essential that libraries develop an induction process through which all job-holders pass. Where possible, the process should be tailored to suit individual needs.

Induction should never be left to chance but should be carefully planned as it will form the foundation on which all other training and working activities are built. During induction the library should demonstrate that it cares for the individual and will encourage the development of new skills and knowledge. A new library assistant may find it frustrating not to be allowed on to the library counter by half past nine on the first day, but an unhurried induction will enable the trainee to feel more confident and relaxed and will ensure that information relating to the skills training is assimilated.

2.1.1 Content of induction programme

For many employees induction will start before the first morning. It will start with the tone of the letter of appointment and subsequent correspondence relating to beginning work. It is essential that all communication is welcoming, clear and precise. There should be no room for confusion – where necessary maps should be sent, names should be clearly identified as should times and room numbers. It is essential that this information is sent out to new staff so that they have time to familiarize themselves with it. However, it can be very useful if the person to whom the new staff member is reporting gives him/her a brief, friendly call shortly before the start date so that any queries can be ironed out and 'the ice broken'.

The content of any induction programme is likely to include basic information about timetables, hours of work, pay arrangements, staff facilities, health and safety, reporting lines, and procedures for reporting illness, as well as a familiarization with the organization and the physical building in which the person will be employed. It is also very useful to state the objectives of the first week so that the trainee is left in no doubt as to what is expected. For example, in an academic library, at the end of week one of the induction programme the new employee should:

- know the layout of the library in which s/he will be working
- know the layout of the campus on which s/he will be based
- be able to reshelve books and journals
- know the colleagues with whom s/he will be working most closely
- have met the chief librarian
- have visited the university's personnel department
- have received and been talked through a staff handbook that details information about conditions of service and pay
- be aware of health and safety requirements
- be familiar with the university's structure and the library's role within it
- have been introduced to the automated system and the range of functions available through it
- be able to issue, return and renew standard items using the computer
- be familiar with the range of duties in which further training will take place and will know the timetable for the next week.

(Adapted from Napier University Library's Training Programme)

It is also very important to remember that staff will need time to take in all this information and wherever possible it should also be presented in written format, usually in the form of an attractive pack with the corporate logo on it. This will not only emphasize the sense of belonging but will give the library assistant a reference to consult, thereby removing some of the pressure to remember everything that is said.

New staff should be made to feel that they are expected: it is no use not putting aside enough time, or having to handle emergencies with a new member of staff in tow. Similarly, this welcome can be conveyed by ensuring that a locker and name badge have been prepared and that the new name appears on appropriate staff lists. This will very quickly convey to the new staff member that s/he is joining a team and will engender a sense of belonging which will ease his/her transition into the new post.

Inadequate induction can give rise later to inefficient performance and the accompanying low motivation and morale which arise from misunderstandings. Good induction can lead to confidence and a sense of well being in the staff member.

The training officer, person responsible for making the appointment or chief librarian is likely to be involved with the induction training, if only from the point of view of offering a library-wide perspective and background to the organization and its policies. One danger to avoid during induction is too much talking, a very easy trap to fall into because the trainer will be very aware of how much the newcomer needs to learn. The needs of the trainee must be of prime consideration and the amount of information given should be limited to manageable sections.

Once the background and welcome have been given it becomes the responsibility of the direct supervisor to introduce the new trainee to the workplace. It is difficult to know exactly where induction ends and job training starts and this is especially true in the area of attitude training.

It is essential that within the induction period new staff learn to adopt an approach conducive to good working relationships with other staff and users. For this reason many authorities cover, during induction, the basic philosophy of public service or, as it is commonly known now, customer care. It is often assumed, erroneously, that this ethos will be readily understood and will require no specific mention. If the new arrival has experience of, and is familiar with, the ideas being presented, then their reiteration merely serves to confirm the library's commitment to the customer focus approach.

2.2 Interpersonal skills

'Interpersonal skills matter because libraries are about people and customer care cannot exist without good interpersonal skills'.[1] The factors outlined in Chapter 1 create stress and strains on staff which can result in it being difficult to maintain pleasant and courteous behaviour. However, many people choose to work in libraries because of the contact with the public, and training in handling interpersonal relationships can ensure that the majority of interactions are positive and satisfactory to all parties. There is a definite relationship between the internal communications and management styles of organizations and its external relations with the public and suppliers. Before an effective customer focus programme can be established it is essential that an effective internal style exists. If this is the case then a 'people' orientation can be established which will pervade all aspects of interpersonal relationships.[2]

Within a customer-focused organization interpersonal skills are central. For this aspect of training to be effective, activities must develop staff and build on their own experiences so that behaviour presented to users looks natural rather than the product of a training package.

2.2.1 *Content of interpersonal skills training*

The exact content and process of interpersonal skills training may vary but certain elements should be included:

*   Essential communication skills: this involves paying close attention to the communication of the speaker through listening, questioning, summarizing and observing body language, facial expressions and general comportment of the individual.
*   Contextual and self awareness: this relates to understanding factors operating in a given situation. These can be cultural differences, issues of gender, race or disability. It is crucial that staff understand that these factors can act subliminally. This is as true within work teams as with library users and it is essential that members of staff endeavour to understand what it is like to be 'in someone else's shoes'. It is only then that the major breakthrough of seeing situations from different perspectives can take place.
*   Teamworking: this generic term applies to behaviour that is essential

not only for satisfactory working relationships with colleagues but also for satisfactory interactions with users. It encompasses the development and maintenance of a trusting atmosphere in which feedback, both positive and negative, can be given and received within a group of staff. An acceptance of feedback will enable the staff member to feel confident in his/her work and in turn has a positive impact on dealings with users. The giving and receiving of feedback, especially negative feedback, is a very difficult skill to acquire and is almost as dependent upon the whole culture of the organization as individual skills. Managers have a responsibility to maintain a trusting, caring work environment in which staff feel comfortable working towards common library objectives and that any feedback should be accepted in that context.

- Assertiveness: this is a topic that has received a very mixed press over the years. Some (often male) senior managers saw it initially as a way in which female staff could become more aggressive. These early misconceptions have faded and there is now a genuine understanding of the value of this technique in handling human interactions. Although valuable in all aspects of work it is particularly useful when handling conflict, refusing unreasonable demands or negotiating change – situations which are now becoming all too familiar within libraries. The main advantage of assertiveness training is in the improved self-esteem and subsequent self confidence that accrue to the individual.

Central to these specific skills is the need for staff to be genuine in their behaviour. Body language must coincide with verbal language and interactions must be rewarding and satisfying for all parties involved.[3] An important element is responsibility; the member of staff must feel a sense of responsibility to the organization, to the job, to colleagues and to users. This may be perceived as 'old fashioned good manners' but, whatever it is called, it is crucial to good working relations because it encompasses punctuality, courteousness, and a respect for others and their feelings.

2.3 Skills training

This will focus on the skills required by an individual to carry out the specific duties of the post. Irrespective of the experience staff bring with them, a detailed training package will be required to enable the duties to be carried out in a manner that allows work to be integrated with other members of the team and the library as a whole.

There may be a desire on the part of the trainee and the employer to start working straight away. It is essential that the training is phased so that self confidence grows and therefore new topics are embraced with ease. Timing is very important. The supervisor or training officer must ensure that s/he understands the process the trainee is undergoing so that changes can be made to the programme without the trainee being made to feel inadequate or unusual.

Initially, it is best to concentrate on essential elements of the duties, with background being introduced later when there is more understanding of the duties and their relationship to the overall work of the library. In most cases the trainee will ask questions that relate to the background aspects of the work through natural interest.

2.3.1 Content of skills training

It is difficult to draw up a definitive list of skills that a new recruit will require because it will be entirely dependent upon the post, the type of library and the experience and background of the trainee.

For counter assistants a basic set of skills can be summarized as:

- Library layout and stock:
  - library layout including special collections
  - shelving, checking, tidying
  - processing stock
  - using the catalogue

- Lending services:
  - circulation procedures (loans, returns, renewals and other associated tasks)
  - registration procedures
  - reservation procedures (receiving requests, handling lists)
  - rules and regulations of the library
  - fines, lost or damaged books (handling cash, giving receipts)
  - interlibrary loan procedures (across the counter)

- Equipment and bookings:
  - photocopiers and other equipment
  - booking procedures for equipment, rooms etc.

- Basic enquiry work:
  - handling simple enquiries
  - referring complex enquiries to appropriate staff.

Within backroom areas such as acquisitions or information systems, job elements will require identification so that suitable training can ensue. For example, in acquisitions the key elements may include:

- bibliographical checking
- order checking and creation
- receipt of stock and invoice passing
- handling stationery requirements
- journal receipt, chasing and administration
- basic cataloguing and indexing.

A full analysis of the job description/specification should have been carried out at the time of advertising and a training needs analysis should be linked to this to ensure that any shift of emphasis in the post is clarified, and appropriate training needs identified.

The training adopted should be clear and logical so that the assistant sees its relevance to the job. If for some reason training on another element of work has to be included, apparently out of sequence, time should be taken to explain its relevance to the overall job and existing training. Such a brief explanation can make a huge difference to the assistant's self confidence because it removes any awkwardness about not making the immediate links.

During this early post-induction phase the trainer should be aware that the trainee may still be lacking confidence and be unaware of interrelationships. For this reason there should be regular feedback sessions with the supervisor or training officer at which progress is monitored in an encouraging, positive atmosphere.

2.4 Bibliographic and reference skills

Any training process can be slow; irrespective of how well it progresses it will be several months before a new member of staff will have as much background knowledge as existing assistants.

If the assistant is to be working at the service desk, then in addition to the job skills it will be valuable to include bibliographic and reference skills, a knowledge of which will enhance the quality of service given across the counter. As the emphasis in library work shifts towards IT it may be inevitable that more library assistants will become involved in some form of basic enquiry work. A new assistant may be anxious to start work in this area as it fulfils the need to 'help people find information', a regularly quoted reason for entering library and information work. Care should be taken to ensure that assistants understand the complexities of information work and know when to refer the enquiry to someone with more expertise in this area.

2.4.1 *Content of bibliographic and reference skills training*

The extent to which individual libraries will use library assistants in reference work will vary enormously depending on the size of the library. However, some basic skills are essential if enquiries are to be answered or referred on competently. For this to happen the two core areas of information sources and techniques of reference interviewing need to be addressed:

- *Information sources* At library assistant level it is essential to know about tools such as the *British national bibliography, Global books in print* and the *Bookseller*. Staff should be trained to locate items within these sources and to interpret the results of the search so that basic enquiries about the availability and cost of stock can be answered. With the advent of these sources on CD-ROM, they are now more accessible to staff at all levels and, as a result of networking, can be available in work areas previously unaccustomed to using them. Traditional sources which library assistants should be introduced to early include encyclopaedias, dictionaries, directories, yearbooks, bibliographies and atlases. Other types of material could be added and sources available in electronic format also need to be closely considered. However, there can be benefits in learning about the basics of information work through looking at traditional sources before transferring that knowledge to electronic formats. The other major categories of information that should be considered are abstracting and indexing services. Many libraries will consider these services within the work of the professionally qualified librarian, nevertheless it is important for library assistants to be aware of their existence and their role in information searching.

  An introduction to the sources should include an understanding of how to assess the value of an individual source, e.g.:

  – currency – when was it published and how is it updated?
  – general or specific subject coverage?

- level – who is its intended readership?
- bias – is there a bias to be considered when evaluating the contents?
- arrangements – is there a specific arrangement which facilitates a
  particular type of enquiry?

In considering these issues it is important to bear in mind the types of questions most regularly asked in a 'quick reference' enquiry – definitions, times, places, methods, people and organizations. It is essential that adequate time is allocated to practising with sample questions as it is only through handling and using materials that library assistants will fully appreciate their value and content.

- *Techniques of reference interviewing* Often questions are phrased in an obscure way and the skills of the reference interviewer will allow an enquiry to be analysed into its constituent parts, thus allowing possible solutions to be identified. This is usually done through careful questioning and prompting. Often the reader will not even be fully aware of what is required. This technique is dependent on the development of effective interpersonal skills.
  The reference interview should identify the problem by ascertaining:

  - what information the user requires
  - how much the user already knows
  - how much information is required and at what level
  - sources already consulted
  - the user's timescale.

Once the basic technique and sources have been mastered, this type of work will become an area of ongoing development as building up a knowledge of alternative sources is fundamental to successful reference work. The library assistant must learn to be flexible in approach and knowledgeable enough to know when to refer the enquirer to someone with more specialist skills and knowledge. The increase in electronic sources is opening up new areas but the same basic techniques will underlie this type of work irrespective of format. It is important when training library assistants that they do not lose sight of the basic elements of reference work in preference to IT solutions.

2.5 Information technology skills

Most library assistants now use IT as an integral part of their daily work and they will learn to use computer systems in a very functional way, often without any real understanding of the systems with which they are working. It is debatable whether all library staff need to be computer literate rather than merely functionally competent. Computer literacy implies a knowledge of the components of a system, being familiar with computer systems and computer programs; being aware of the uses and potential of IT, and understanding the trends in IT and the social implications of widespread use. While such an understanding may be desirable it may not be appropriate for all staff.[4] Its relevance will be dependent upon the size and type of library. At this stage it will be necessary to identify which core skills need to be covered by all staff, and the particular tasks specialists will be required to carry out. The Library Association's bid to the Millennium

Fund to link all public libraries to the Internet[5] could rapidly change the nature of service provision and the skills associated with delivering it.

The area of IT training may also raise 'techno-fears' in some staff, particularly, but not exclusively, in older members of staff. If this occurs care must be taken to build up confidence in using the equipment and systems. This can be a slow process but is best achieved through regular and frequent contact with the systems.

2.5.1 Content of information technology skills training

For a library assistant working at the counter it may be assumed that an ability to work competently with the following areas will be required:

- within the automated system – circulation control
- online public access catalogue (OPAC) searching and an understanding of the relationships between constituent databases
- interrogating acquisitions and serials modules
- basic troubleshooting with computer equipment – maintenance of printers etc.
- upgrading catalogue records
- awareness of online searching and CD-ROM technology
- awareness of specialist electronic sources
- word processing and keyboard skills
- electronic mail (if used).

2.6 Continuing self development within the organization

Following induction and basic skills training it is essential for staff to learn how their work contributes to the wider organization and how they will be expected to develop within their jobs. The 'environment' in which staff work on a day-to-day basis should be supportive and conducive to learning. This ambience will derive from the attitude of senior staff, who must be seen to be supportive of training and personal and procedural improvement.

Bennis and Nanus[6] characterize this atmosphere by emphasizing the need for service leadership. Service leadership derives from an 'understanding and emphasis on emotional and spiritual resources of an organization, whereas managers emphasize physical resources such as raw materials, technology and capital'. The essence of 'service leadership' is an atmosphere in which staff are not over managed – supervisors are seen in the midst of the action rather than behind their desks. It is from this position that they can work alongside their staff – mentoring, coaching, praising, listening, talking. This creates a dialogue in which a 'sense of team' is created and staff can fulfil their investment in training to the benefit of the library service and their own job satisfaction. Staff need to learn how to work effectively as team members. True team working is about much more than just working alongside each other. It encompasses objective setting, maintaining motivation, communication, reviewing work and resolving possible conflict to achieve stated objectives.[7]

The move towards flatter organizations in which 'managers' support and facilitate the work of their colleagues seems to be incorporating the essence of service leadership and improved service but for this to be effective changes in organizational culture and attitudes need to be achieved. Have library managers had the training to achieve these changes?

2.7 Supervisory training

Changes in organizational structures are resulting in teams being led by senior library assistants who increasingly need training in supervisory and basic management skills. Before moving on to supervisory skills, a library assistant must have proven experience with the skills already identified within library routines, IT and interpersonal skills. In addition they must have a thorough working understanding of the objectives of the organization and the preferred methods of achieving these.

2.7.1 *Content of supervisory training*

Essential to any supervisory skills course is the acceptance that the job involves responsibilities for other staff and processes. Basic elements which should be included are:

- managing people: getting staff to work together; getting the best from staff members; managing absence; handling conflict; general employment issues
- finance: sources of funding; budget breakouts; folio headings; budgetary control
- communication: appropriate oral and written communication; explaining current issues and developments to staff; chairing team meetings; identifying when and how to take issues forward; casemaking
- time management: for the individual and the team; work planning, organization and timetabling
- delegation: decision making; problem solving
- training methods: including counselling, coaching and feedback methods.

References

1 Mills, S., *Interpersonal skills training manual*, London, TFPL, 1993.
2 Levy, P., *Interpersonal skills*, London, Library Association Publishing, 1993.
3 Jordon, P., 'Training in handling users', in Prytherch, R. (ed.), *Handbook of library training practice*, Aldershot, Gower, 1986.
4 Lantz, B., 'Staff training for information technology', *British journal of academic librarianship*, **2** (1), 1987, 44–64.
5 Dobson, P., 'Bid for a virtual monument', *Library Association record*, **98** (2), 1996, 84–5.
6 Bennis, W. and Nanus, B., *Leaders: their strategies for taking charge*, New York, Harper & Row, 1985.
7 Bluck, R., *Team management*, London, Library Association Publishing, 1996.

3 Delivery methods

3.1 Background

From the employer's point of view any training given to staff must ensure that investment of time and effort pays off quickly and offers added value to the service being provided. This can present problems where horizons are short term as training benefits are almost always long term. For that reason it is important that the training adopted is the most appropriate both for the library and the library assistant. This requires the person overseeing the process to have a basic understanding of learning styles and how they relate to individuals' needs and the resources available.

There is no single correct way of training new or existing staff: a range of methods can be used but whichever is adopted it is crucial that four factors are borne in mind:

- the method chosen should be appropriate to the task in hand
- the training should be well prepared and free from interruptions
- it should be kept as simple as possible
- it should achieve its stated objectives.

Bearing in mind these basic tenets there are different approaches which can be used successfully with the types of training already outlined.

During induction it will have been possible to gather information, both formally and informally, about the library assistant's past experience and knowledge and it is important that this prior learning is acknowledged. It may not be directly applicable but it may indicate a basic understanding of routines and library practice which can facilitate the teaching of other tasks.

Motivation is the other important consideration in the successful retention and utilization of training. Motivation will also be influenced by the outcomes associated with the learning. If the outcomes of successful learning lead to enhanced job satisfaction, opportunities to do different work, increased pay or promotion possibilities, then a higher level of motivation will exist than if the outcomes are perceived as negative or threatening. The trainer must be aware of the trainee's needs and create a supportive and psychologically safe learning environment in which the trainee will become actively involved in the process. The retention of information is closely linked to the individual's preferred learning style and therefore the trainer should try to vary the delivery to facilitate the trainee's learning. It is as important to consider the individual's ability to retain and use knowledge as it is to impart it in an appropriate way.

3.2 Planning

Careful planning is the key to successful training and if consideration is given to the following four basic questions then a structure will be imposed on the sessions which will benefit both the trainee and the trainer.[1]

3.2.1 *Who?*

The training officer may not be the most knowledgeable person to convey certain routines and it may be necessary to use an experienced library assistant. However, if this is done care must be taken to ensure that the information is given in a clear, concise manner. Library assistants who will be involved with training new staff should be closely associated with the whole process in order that they understand their role in the training programme and are not working in isolation. Training should always be undertaken by someone who is reliable, patient, thorough and has had some basic instruction in training methods.

3.2.2 *What?*

It can be very valuable to consider on-the-job training as a series of specific objectives, such as: *At the end of this training session the trainee will be able to issue and return books using the automated issue system.* Behind such an objective lie many other factors which will need clarification. For example, how will the trainee know how to handle any messages or blocks that appear on the screen? In that case there is a series of sub-objectives which can be identified prior to training. The advantage of this approach is that it can easily be monitored by the trainee and the supervisor and regular feedback on progress can be given. The use of checklists often accompanies this approach.

3.2.3 *Where?*

The location of equipment and workspaces often determines where training takes place. Wherever possible the location chosen should be free from interruption and conducive to learning. The ideal solution is to have a training suite which can be booked for appropriate periods. Such an area should have access to the automated system and other sources and equipment required for a range of library activities. This would enable demonstration and practice to be carried out in a 'safe' if slightly artificial environment. For some activities, such as role-play or interpersonal skills, the normal workplace would be wholly inappropriate but the application of such training could take place under supervision during a normal work session. In large authorities it is a good idea to have the training undertaken in one large library to ensure a standardized approach while also giving rise to more activity and opportunities to see unusual or infrequent occurrences

3.2.4 *When?*

Timing must be dictated by the needs of the service and the readiness of the trainee. It is important that sufficient planning goes into the training to ensure that trainer and trainee can be available together with the necessary equipment. While some aspects may best be left for an external course many others should be carried out in-house as required. Over time the training officer will build up sufficient experience to gauge the appropriate time for training to take place. It is important to ensure that previous training has been assimilated and used effectively before introducing new topics.

3.3 Internal or external?

It is worth considering the range of activities which fall into each of these categories in order to assess their effectiveness. Some employees may not acknowledge training that takes place at work – for many people 'proper' training involves attendance at a course. However, with careful support and guidance possibly the most valuable training takes place as part of the normal work routine. Internal training methods are those which take place within the library and utilize the skills of the library staff. External training will involve the staff member attending training sessions away from the normal workplace, frequently with external trainers and normally alongside trainees from other libraries.

On-the-job training is aimed at improving a member of staff's ability to deal with the workload on a personal, daily basis. For a more comprehensive coverage such training can be supplemented by other activities – preferably away from work so that daily routines can be looked at objectively.

Internal	*External*
'Sitting next to Nellie'	Cooperative training
Off-the-job training	Staff exchanges and secondments
Workshops and seminars	Supplier training
Reading or self-instructional materials	Specialist or non-library training courses
Coaching, mentoring and counselling	

3.3.1 *Internal training*

'Sitting next to Nellie'
Seeing and doing are powerful tools and therefore 'sitting next to Nellie' survives as one of the most effective methods for communicating on-the-job training. For this process to be truly effective it is necessary to build in elements of practice and testing to ensure that what is being shown is understood and retained by the trainee. Such training should be carried out in an appropriate environment where there is sufficient time to explain procedures and practices without the immediate pressure of being watched by library users. Levels of competence should be adequate prior to trainees being exposed to users and frequently this can be achieved through explanatory training sessions with exercises, interspersed with time at the service desks. It has the advantage of giving immediate feedback so that the learning process is enhanced through a dialogue of encouragement and correction.

Despite its many advantages there are inherent pitfalls in this approach to which the supervisor must be alert. Lack of preparation can result in the trainer not knowing what is expected. This can result in too much detail being imparted during one session. It is also essential that 'Nellie' is a competent trainer and well briefed by the training officer about the trainee's past experience, motivation and approach.

Off-the-job training
Off-the-job training within the library may be presented in the form of sim-

ulations or role plays, and works best where a group of staff can be brought together for half a day, or more. The advantage is that it creates a setting in which trainees can experiment free from interruptions. A skilled group leader who can ensure that the group 'gels' is essential to the success of these sessions. The result can be an enhancement of the trainees' self confidence as well as knowledge. Such sessions can be useful for interpersonal skills or reference skills (see Appendix 1).

Workshops and seminars

Workshops are similar to off-the-job training but tend to involve practical skills development, typically with hands-on practice which will be supervised and commented upon. It is particularly valuable in the area of information technology where the workshop may in fact be a PC laboratory in which trainees can experiment with automated modules, new pieces of equipment, CD-ROMs or electronic mail. Such sessions allow a relaxed atmosphere to develop in which the trainer adopts the role of facilitator by offering immediate feedback. It is important to ensure that the trainee is given adequate opportunity after the session to practise.

The strength of seminars lies in the dissemination and discussion of policies to ensure thorough understanding. Their use with library assistants should be sparing as they will be less involved with policy determination and issues. However, as all library staff will be involved with implementing policies and interpreting them to users, it is important that a thorough understanding is gained. In the case of library assistants this might be achieved more effectively through team meetings.

Reading or self-instructional materials

All or any of the preceding methods can be supplemented by reading or self-instructional materials. The development and use of such materials can ease the training process as it provides a framework into which practical sessions are inserted. Careful selection of these materials is required. An objectives approach can assist in determining their focus. It is important that the trainee understands how these materials support or complement other training sessions so that appropriate associations are made.

The major advantage of in-house pre-prepared printed materials is that trainees can build up their own resource of training materials which can be referred to whenever necessary. It will also allow the trainee to work alone and will contribute to a sense of independence (see Appendix 2).

Each of these methods will be strengthened and reinforced if coaching, mentoring and counselling form an integral part of the training practice.

Coaching, mentoring and counselling

Coaching is the practice of turning work incidents into learning experiences and is best carried out by the trainee's supervisor. It involves examining in more detail incidents as they occur and considering whether the situation could have been handled differently. This allows the trainee to see a more positive approach to the incident. It is very much the opportunity for a more experienced member of staff to contribute his/her knowledge in a positive and supportive manner. A learning log can be used as a prompt in coaching sessions and can help trainees reconsider incidents and turn them into learning experiences (see Appendix 3).

'A mentor is a more experienced individual, willing to share his/her knowledge with someone less experienced in a relationship of mutual trust'.[2] Mentors can help staff members to assimilate training and new experiences through giving constructive feedback and acting as a sounding board for ideas and emotions. They also play a crucial role in smoothing the path of a new employee especially in terms of how to get things done within a large organization. A mentor can act as an organizational signpost, highlighting the best routes to achieve success. (See Appendix 4). Although frequently considered with a new member of staff, a mentoring relationship can also prove worthwhile whenever a member of staff moves into a new area of work or is perceived to require some additional support. The emotional support a mentor offers should never be underestimated. Research[3] shows that careful mentoring can have real benefits for the organization, the individual employee and the mentor.

Counselling is similar to coaching but is more likely to result directly from some of the trainee's work being monitored. It is essential that work is checked following training to ensure that it has been understood and assimilated. The trainee should be aware that work will be monitored and commented upon until such time as the supervisor is satisfied that an acceptable standard has been achieved. This process is critical to successful training outcomes as it provides a method of ensuring that the training has been effective. Without this confirmation the training may have been to no avail.

3.3.2 *External training*

Although initial library training needs to be carried out internally there is a distinctive role for external training. It can provide the opportunity to come into contact with a range of new ideas and approaches from a new set of colleagues. Care should be taken when using external courses to ensure that a trainee will benefit from attendance. Transfer and application of learning can be difficult and assistance may be required. New relationships have to be established quickly and there may also be issues of direct costs related to attendance fees and travel. Of these, perhaps the transfer of learning is the issue on which to concentrate most carefully. The course objectives should be considered in order to assess their relevance to the trainee. Most external courses will aim to attract an adequate audience and therefore their publicity may be written in such a way as to give the impression that the course will be all things to all trainees. If necessary, the organizers should be contacted and the content discussed in more detail to ascertain its value. It can be demoralizing for the trainee to attend training that is at the wrong level or approached in an unfamiliar way.

Cooperative training

This acts almost as a hybrid of internal/external training as it will be organized by training officers within a group of participating libraries, thus there is direct input relating to organizational requirements. There is a generally held view that both cooperation and training are 'good things' and therefore cooperative training should be doubly good.[4] Undoubtedly there are economies of scale to be achieved which result in such presentations being more efficient: these will appeal to the management aspects of training. However, for the individual the benefits are less well proven. Careful preparation and debriefing may be required to ensure that the training is related to an individual's workplace. Such sessions are better suited to experienced staff as they are most successful when considering comparative work practices.

Cooperative training on interpersonal skills and reference skills at library assistant level can be very valuable. Much can be gained by bringing a diverse group of staff together to share such issues. These sessions can act as a 'safety valve' for staff by making them realize that their concerns are usually shared by others. Simply giving them the opportunity to spend a few hours focusing on one or two issues can boost confidence and return the trainee to the workplace feeling 'recharged'. On return this enthusiasm must be managed carefully so that new ideas are carefully considered and shared with supervisors. Failure to do so can result in disenchantment and a questioning of the value of attendance at training courses.

Recently another management issue which has arisen within certain organizations is the need to be financially accountable for training offered on a cooperative basis: in some instances it is perceived that smaller institutions have much to gain but not much to contribute in such an arrangement. These factors are impacting on the Access to Libraries for Learning scheme (ALL) which is run by the Learners and Researchers Group of SINTO (Sheffield Interchange Organization) in Sheffield.[5] These factors are less important when all the participating organizations are seen as equal, as is the case with the East Midlands Academic Libraries and Information Services in Cooperation (EMALINK). This group successfully organizes a programme of cooperative training but to date little has been aimed specifically at library assistants, although clearly the infrastructure exists (see Appendix 5).

Staff exchanges and secondments
An interesting element of cooperative training is staff exchange and secondment. These can be difficult to organize because of differences in conditions of service, and senior management may be reluctant to have staff out of the library for lengthy periods of time. It also imposes additional pressures on the remaining staff because of the need to carry out basic training and orientation. It is essential when organizing such an exchange that the trainee's objectives are identified in conjunction with the training officer and clearly understood by all concerned. Within a large authority or multi-campus university library it may be possible to arrange exchanges to other parts of the library. For example, a counter assistant can learn much about the overall service by spending time in the acquisitions section and vice versa. The immediate hurdles of such a temporary move should be overcome for the benefit of the individual and the organization. A fuller understanding of the system can contribute directly to a better service across the counter. Many larger authorities now regard regular transfers to other sections as an integral part of in-house training.

In addition to the formalized cooperative training existing between organizations, training is organized by local LA branches or groups. As with cooperative training, it is likely that various interested libraries will be represented. However, individuals on organizing committees may be in a less advantageous position to advise on training needs. A survey of the Calendar in the *Library Association record* indicates that branches and groups tend to react to current issues rather than identifiable training needs. This can create overlap and duplication, resulting in poor attendance at individual sessions. In Scotland one reaction to this has been the creation of the Groups and Branches Day at the Scottish Library Association's Annual Conference. This allows staff at all levels to attend a range of seminars organized by local groups, for a modest fee, and is regarded as a day for all those who work in libraries.

Supplier training
As mentioned in the section on IT training, suppliers often provide training in new systems modules. Some library authorities may decide that this is best presented to senior staff for onward transmission to staff. However, benefits can accrue from staff being trained at first hand and when buying new equipment, software or systems attention should be paid to the training package that is included. Direct training of the staff who will be using it can be beneficial as they can receive direct answers to their queries and have the opportunity for supervised practice. Such direct training can cover automated systems, CD-ROM services, photocopiers and reader printers, specialist equipment for special needs' users, security systems, laminators, faxes and other types of office equipment.

Specialist or non-library training courses
On occasion, library staff can benefit from joining courses not directly aimed at library personnel. These may encompass such areas as finance, conservation, health and safety, stationery purchasing supplies, IT, interpersonal skills and environmental issues. The benefits which accrue from these are broadly similar to those gained from attendance at other external courses, the main problem again being the links to be made from the course to the work situation. For that reason, such courses are primarily of value to experienced library assistants, or those aiming to become senior library assistants.

References

1   Blanksby, M., *Staff training: a librarian's handbook*, Newcastle-under-Lyne, AAL Publishing, 1988.
2   Clutterbuck, D., *Mentoring kit*, Henley Distance Learning Ltd, 1992.
3   Clutterbuck, D., *Everyone needs a mentor: fostering talent at work*, 2nd edn, London, Institute of Personnel Management, 1991.
4   Baker, D., 'Co-operative training: the academic libraries perspective', in MacDougall, A. and Prytherch, R., *Co-operative training in libraries*, Aldershot, Gower, 1989.
5   'ALL is launched – now the work really begins', *SINTO newsletter*, **1**, June 1996.

4 Educational opportunities

4.1 Levels of work

The balance between training, development and education within librarianship has been difficult to define and distinguish over the years. Before the advent of an all-graduate profession, the three tended to merge to produce a qualified librarian. Those who did not complete the Library Association (LA) examinations usually passed the first professional (or entrance) examinations, which employers took as a basic level of competence.

There is still a confusion between the levels of work that are carried out within libraries. Many within the profession have failed to accept that there is a role for recognized paraprofessionals whose work output is defined in general terms by a professional but who is at liberty to use a number of procedures or skills to achieve the objectives. For the paraprofessional this provides a degree of freedom, within set boundaries, to carry out work in the manner s/he considers best. This can provide for the professional a well executed, often imaginatively presented piece of work. The library assistant, on the other hand, can normally be expected to carry out work according to specific instructions and in a recognized and established manner.

The widening of higher education brought with it degree courses in librarianship which the LA quickly recognized as the way to maintain professional status. Unfortunately in the rush towards an all-graduate profession, library assistants fell behind.

4.2 Courses available

City and Guilds
The City and Guilds Certificate for Library and Information Assistants (737) is a one-year course and is the longest running of the paraprofessional qualifications, having been established in the UK during the 1960s. A new syllabus is proposed for 1997 but the current certificate is comprehensive and provides a good foundation for library assistants. It is a competence-based vocational qualification and therefore most colleges prefer candidates to be in employment so that practical work and assessments can be undertaken. Over the years there has been considerable debate about its content and value but it is currently undergoing a revival, largely because it is being linked closely with the Underpinning Knowledge and Understanding (UKU) required for S/NVQs and it is hoped that the forthcoming changes will further complement this work.

BTEC courses
The syllabus for the BTEC Certificate of Achievement in Library and Information Work is determined by the centre delivering it and therefore

can be more responsive to local needs. In level it is broadly similar to the Scottish Vocational Education Council (SCOTVEC) Higher Certificate and it encourages analysis through work-related assignments. It can be taken as a course on its own but is more commonly studied as an option module as the BTEC National Certificate in Business and Finance. This qualification provides a wider context that some library assistants find valuable, especially if working within a local authority. Its content and assignment work can also be used as UKU and evidence for NVQs. This BTEC module is no longer offered in distance learning mode by the public sector trade union, UNISON.

College certificates
Having completed the Library and Information Certificate (LAIC) many library assistants, particularly those working in specific areas of librarianship, feel they want to continue their studies. These modules or courses are usually validated by colleges or educational federations and can be used as part of a wider qualification or as an end in themselves. Entry will vary depending on the specific course but work experience within a specific sector or an educational qualification is normally required. Topics currently available include Management for Senior Library Assistants, Running a School Library, User Education in Libraries, and Open Learning in Public Libraries (see Appendix 9).

SCOTVEC courses
Two courses run in Scotland under the auspices of SCOTVEC. The certificate course is at a basic level (broadly comparable to LAIC) and many authorities use it as a basic introduction to library work and further education. The higher certificate course is primarily aimed at those with three or four years' work experience and who are interested in the 'why' of librarianship. It is therefore more academically challenging than the certificate course. Although the qualification is Scottish, an ever-increasing number of candidates from England and Northern Ireland are undertaking these courses by distance learning as no equivalent qualification is delivered in that mode.

Degree courses
Many library assistants gain a great deal from studying at certificate level and want to continue their studies to degree level as this offers the possibility of admission to the Professional Register.

Universities are increasingly open to 'non-standard' entry qualifications and mature candidates with relevant vocational qualifications (as listed above) plus good work experience are normally given advanced standing, although each case will be considered on its own merits. Most degree programmes are still run in full-time mode but an increasing number are considering part-time study or participation in the Credit Accumulation and Transfer Scheme (CATS). For many library assistants these flexible modes are more appropriate as domestic responsibilities or financial pressures may make full time study impossible. Only the University of Wales at Aberystwyth currently offers a distance learning degree programme and it is proving both popular and successful. Some library assistants choose to study for a first degree with the Open University and then proceed to a postgraduate qualification, many more of which are available part time.

4.3 Course content

The content of courses has always been subject to some controversy. Moves towards competence-based qualifications have meant that course content normally achieves an acceptable balance between theory and practice.

The main components of the LAIC and the SCOTVEC certificate courses include:

- libraries and their role within society
- interpersonal behaviour and communication
- stock selection, storage and maintenance
- organizing information, including cataloguing, classification and indexing
- service provision for library users
- sources of information and information retrieval.

In all aspects of these courses computers are accepted as a major component and information technology applications are studied as appropriate.

Most aspects of these syllabuses require the students to describe, explain or carry out procedures and routines and as such offer an education appropriate to a range of tasks, most of which will be routine and non-complex.

The level of the SCOTVEC Higher Certificate and the BTEC Certificate are more accurately described as being at paraprofessional level and require candidates to compare, evaluate and differentiate the materials, which involves consideration of the implications of the procedures and services. These courses also include studying aspects of finance, personnel and other managerial issues. An important element is the form of assessments which can allow candidates to bring together disparate elements of the course and link them to the practicalities of the workplace. Projects or case studies allow able library assistants to work independently to demonstrate their skills of analysis and synthesis.

The Higher Certificate can lead into degree level work and topics are explored in more detail and with more analysis. Managerial and computing aspects are also given more prominence. It is normal practice in degree programmes to give students the opportunity to study related topics such as literature, media studies or sociology. This has the advantage of giving library assistants a wider perspective on the role of libraries and information in society.

4.4 Delivery mechanisms

The effective delivery of vocational education demands flexibility and a variety of routes is available through colleges:

- full-time attendance
- part-time, day release attendance
- distance learning supported by telephone tutorials and in-college weeks
- block-release full-time attendance (normally offered to those not in employment)
- fax delivery, where students are given a fax machine for the duration of the course (an innovative method pioneered by Somerset College of Arts and Technology).

Contact should be made with the relevant examining bodies to ascertain which centres offer courses and in which modes. Not all centres offer all modes and the distance learning modes prove particularly popular because of the flexibility that is offered to both employee and employer. They also enable theory and practice to come together within the workplace. Problems associated with releasing staff to attend colleges have been addressed by some local authorities such as Gateshead,[1] which developed an in-house City and Guilds course to meet particular service needs.

4.5 Practical or theoretical?

The relevance of course attendance, in addition to in-house training, is evinced by the fact that an awareness of, and involvement in, wider issues can serve to motivate staff, which in turn contributes to a general improvement in service provision. Employers who are committed to the profession, the service and their employees will appreciate the benefits to be gained by supporting staff through courses of education.

A balance between the theoretical and the practical must be maintained if the content is to be relevant to library assistants and their employers. Irrespective of the level of study or training, it must be remembered that library work is practical and in order to carry it out effectively library staff must gain experience based on good in-house training and complemented by appropriate theoretical background.

4.6 Trainers' support groups

Within most organizations there will be only one person responsible for training policy and therefore on occasions the role can seem isolated. Much benefit can be gained through exchanging experience with counterparts in other libraries and also with course providers. Where cooperative training ventures exist this type of discussion normally takes place. The Association for the Education and Training of Library Technicians and Assistants (AETLTA) also provides a forum.[2]

AETLTA operates as an organization in liaison with the LA and it brings together course tutors and training officers. It aims through discussions to arrive at the best possible training opportunities. As more authorities become involved in S/NVQs this forum will provide a valuable source of support and shared experience.

References

1   Photograph and caption, *Library Association record,* **97** (9), 1995, 507.
2   Williamson, M., 'Training: it's good to talk, a letter to the editor', *Library Association record,* **98** (7), 1996, 349.

5 Scottish and National Vocational Qualifications (S/NVQs)

5.1 Introduction

An employer needs to know that an employee can carry out certain tasks competently and consistently within the workplace. To that end the employer must accept responsibility for ensuring that opportunities for training exist. The overriding characteristic of the training and education described so far is that it deals with inputs and methodologies, not outcomes. As a result there is no way of anticipating how effectively a trainee will be able to perform once the training has been completed. Other issues of concern to employees and employers alike is the increasing difficulty of releasing staff to attend courses – as a result of either staff shortages or decreases in training budgets. The increase in flexible learning opportunities has gone some way to alleviating this problem. By their nature standard courses are intended to have a wide appeal and while individual experiences are intended to bring course content to life, for many employees the information provided is not immediately relevant to individual needs or local circumstances. For others, training or education may not be feasible because of the part-time nature of employment: it seems certain that part-time and temporary contracts are set to stay and this category of 'flexible' workers, frequently women returners, may miss out on basic and developmental training, let alone education for progression or advancement.

5.2 Development of S/NVQs

These issues are not exclusive to libraries and over the past few years a national system of competence-based vocational qualifications has enabled employers to address many of these issues.

National Vocational Qualifications or Scottish Vocational Qualifications present the employer with a method of recognizing skills while allowing employees to take control of their own development. S/NVQs allow employees to demonstrate their ability to carry out the tasks related to a job, irrespective of whether they are school leavers, graduates or library workers with extensive experience. They should complement in-house training or education and allow a formal qualification to be achieved. Credit is given for doing a job well and this credit can be transferred to another post, another employer or indeed another area of employment.

Through extensive discussions with practitioners, the lead body has developed a set of standards for the profession from which competencies can be assessed. These standards can be of value within libraries even if candidates do not enter for assessment as they comprise a manual of good work practice that is on-going in libraries. As part of the quality assurance system there is a commitment to keep the standards up-to-date by periodic revision. This will mean that the standards issued in mid-1995 will be reviewed by mid-1998. The standards are recognized throughout the United Kingdom andthe European Union and increasingly further afield.

S/NVQs are available in five levels but within the Library and Information Services there are currently only three available, levels 2, 3 and 4. Level 5 is being developed. Care has been taken to ensure that the levels are comparable across different sectors and units can be transferred from one sector to another as appropriate. For example, customer care is applicable across a range of other units and has not been written specifically for library work. Instead it will be the responsibility of the trainee to demonstrate that s/he has the competencies required to achieve the qualification within his/her own particular workplace.

5.3   Levels of S/NVQs

Level 2, currently the first level for Library and Information Services, is 'intended for library assistants'.[1] It covers processing materials, identifying and providing information and working with users. Achievement at this level requires competence in a number of varied activities within a range of contexts. This level could broadly be deemed to equate to the level of the certificate courses identified in Chapter 4.

Level 3 is intended 'for senior library assistants or information officers'[1] and covers providing information, organizing information, solving problems for users and maintaining quality standards. In addition to the mandatory units, candidates must complete five optional units which cover user services, information technology and processing, and supervising activities. The majority of activities included in this level will be complex and non-routine and will require some independent judgement.

Level 4 is intended for 'librarians, customer services managers or information managers'[1] and encompasses units on identifying strategy for meeting users' needs, determining information requirements, planning displays and maintaining and improving quality. This level encompasses technical and professional tasks involving personal responsibility and autonomy to resolve complex tasks.

When considered against the categories of work identified in Chapter 4 similarities of level can be seen.[1]

5.4   Competence and self responsibility

S/NVQs differ from the methods already discussed because they consider specifically competence at work – staff are judged against national standards on their ability to do a real job in the workplace. This guarantees that they are relevant and comparable across different workplaces, and even across different sectors. Another major difference is the importance that the scheme places on self-responsibility – it is incumbent upon the employee, with guidance, to identify training gaps and to organize ways in which they can be filled. If candidates can demonstrate they have met these standards they are awarded the qualification.

5.5   Gaining S/NVQs

Prior to enrolling with his/her local assessment centre the candidate should undertake a self-assessment of readiness to enter a particular level. This self-assessment is available through the Royal Society of Arts (RSA) or SCOTVEC. A variety of organizations are being established as assessment centres ranging from large authorities to local colleges of further education, individual consultants and other local consortia which may comprise organizations too small to support the whole assessment process alone. Although not established as assessment centres themselves, the RSA, SCOTVEC and local training and enterprise centres can be instrumental in establishing centres.

Surrey County Libraries was the first local authority to become an assessment centre. John Hobson[2] is on record as stating his pleasure with the NVQ approach as being the way forward with making developmental training available to all library assistant staff. Before Surrey, Somerset College of Arts and Technology,[3] which has a long-standing background of para-professional education, became the first assessment centre in the country to be validated for the delivery of ILS-NVQs. They opted for a consortium approach partly because it has financial advantages for the college but also because it can be used as a centre for the assessor qualifications. This removes the immediate necessity of all organizations which offer NVQs to be set up validation centres and train their own assessors. It also leaves individual organizations with the option of becoming independent of the college at a later stage when their own NVQ provision is further developed.

This cooperative approach, at least at this early stage of implementation, would seem to be an economical and advantageous use of a central resource. Such an approach may also re-awaken interest in cooperative training in areas where it has been struggling to survive. There is also potential in using Library Information Plans, and an example of this is Bedford and Buckinghamshire Information (BBI) which uses Cranfield University as its centre.

In addition to colleges of further education being established as assessment centres universities are also becoming involved. The Department of Information and Library Management at the University of Northumbria at Newcastle[4] in conjunction with the Northern Training Group became the first school of librarianship to be involved as an assessment centre. The Department is confident that its involvement will help to raise the profile of NVQs within the profession while ensuring that the education being delivered is both vocationally and educationally sound.[5] The increase in accreditation of prior learning (APL), coupled with the range of levels encompassed by the ILS-NVQs makes this seem probable.

Once enrolled at the assessment centre an assessor will be assigned who can help the candidate to identify evidence that will have to be gathered prior to assessment. It is likely that a mentor (sometimes also known as adviser or tutor) will also be assigned. This person will act as a sounding board for ideas and offer guidance and advice during the collection of evidence. Candidates will be given a Cumulative Assessment Record (CAR) which is a copy of all the units that comprise the S/NVQ. The CAR will form a check as to the variety and range of evidence that is required for each unit and for each S/NVQ.

5.5.1 *The assessor*

The assessor will be a knowledgeable and competent person with extensive and current working experience within the same field and therefore will be capable of judging the adequacy and quality of the evidence. It will be the assessor who decides whether the evidence submitted is sufficient to demonstrate competence. There are inbuilt safeguards: each centre has internal verifiers who ensure that assessments are verified across the centre; external verifiers, approved by the lead body and paid for by the awarding bodies, approve and inspect centres and also have the power to withdraw approval. Assessments are also verified across the country to ensure that S/NVQ standards are consistent from one centre to another. The responsibility for ensuring that assessors are properly trained to offer candidates informed and competent advice also falls on the external assessors.

5.5.2   *The documentation*

There are two main aspects to the documentation:

- Materials produced by the lead body which clearly identify the competence. Each qualification consists of a number of *units of competence*, some of which are mandatory and some of which are optional. Units are made up of *elements of competence*. Within each element there are *performance criteria* which indicate the required standards of performance. The contexts of performance are set out in *range statements*. Each element also indicates essential *underpinning knowledge and understanding*. (See Appendix 7 for an example of a unit). For many candidates the language of competence-based assessment and the idea of building a portfolio are new and most assessment centres run introductory sessions on S/NVQs and on portfolio building to overcome these initial difficulties. Library assistants, once familiar with the language, usually find level 2 relatively straightforward to achieve. Many experience some difficulty in making the transition to level 3 because it involves more responsibility and autonomy.
- The information a candidate will need to compile and present as evidence. This falls into two main categories: firstly, the performance evidence, which must include observation and products such as reports, memos, letters, or photographs of displays etc. that have been involved in producing part of the work; secondly, the supplementary evidence, often obtained through questioning, probing and observing. The assessor may use these methods to ensure that any evidence presented which is more than three years old is still relevant.

The candidate must present his/her own case as proof that s/he is worthy of being awarded the competence. To be acceptable the evidence must be sufficient – that is, it must cover the ground, it must be current (normally evidence will be presented within three years), and it must have been achieved within the appropriate work environment.

5.5.3   *The portfolio*

In addition to the evidence presented, the portfolio should include a current CV, job description, details of the work organization and support that has been forthcoming from mentors, assessors or employers. In essence it should be presented in a manner similar to a major project, with a title page, table of contents, and glossary of specific terms used throughout the portfolio. Once compiled, the portfolio will be a body of evidence that can be presented to prospective employers as a summary of achievements and abilities. 'A well organized portfolio, containing well-selected evidence arranged in a clear and easily understood way, immediately says something important and relevant about its owner. After all, organizing information for easy retrieval is at the heart of what information work is all about!'⁵

The portfolio should be retained throughout a career as it may be used as evidence in achieving more than one unit.

5.6 Implications for the candidate

This scheme places a great deal of responsibility on the trainees to achieve the units; it will require the trainee to be self-motivated, methodical, dedicated and organized. The scheme should help to encourage good interpersonal skills, written and organizational skills which many of the traditional courses have striven to achieve, sometimes through contrived methods. The scheme allows the employee to work at his/her own pace. This will be unaffected by whether employment is full-time, part-time, paid or voluntary or is interrupted by maternity leave or other lengthy breaks. The documentation emphasizes self development aspects while stressing the importance of gaining recognition for individual skills within a particular level. S/NVQs clearly identify different grades of ability and individual skills within grade and therefore present detailed knowledge about an individual's ability. It seems likely that there will be a wider use of standards for framing job descriptions for use in performance review interviews and many employers may regard them as the method by which rewards (financial or through promotion) are made to staff.

5.7 Implications for the employer

The scheme allows staff to gain a nationally recognized qualification for work that is being carried out as part of his/her normal routines. The major responsibility will lie with the employee to gather evidence. The all important mentoring or support role, which should be present in all organizations, is given a formal standing, with the employee being in a position to request support from supervisors. For many employees, working for S/NVQs will clarify their thinking and make them more reflective about their work. This should impact positively on the service provision. In addition, if they feel their skills and worth are being acknowledged they will probably be more responsive to users, thus ultimately improving the service. A major factor will be the desire on the part of some employees to gain units in areas not normally associated with their work and therefore requesting experience in situations not usually considered their own. The expressed needs of individuals will require careful management if they are to comply with organizational aims and objectives.

There may be more demand to attend in-house training courses in order to gain the relevant background information about an aspect of the service. This is likely to lead to an enhanced and extended provision of training by employers that will satisfy S/NVQs requirements. Likewise, interest in the traditional educational courses may increase as employees realize their need to have supporting knowledge and understanding.

The development of candidate support materials, such as the commercially produced FastTrack materials (see Useful Addresses), or other open learning products to support, in particular, the UKU, will allow preparations for S/NVQs to become independent of college-based courses thus allowing them to be achieved within the workplace.

5.8 Costs

It is difficult to estimate the cost of taking an ILS-NVQ as it will depend upon the level of qualification and the evidence which will be required to fill the identified gaps. The lead body is currently suggesting a cost of £250–£950 per qualification, the actual figure being dependent upon the assessment required.

5.9 Other considerations

The entire ethos of S/NVQs, where the emphasis is on self-development and gaining recognition for the skills acquired as part of the normal workload, helps to strengthen the notion discussed in the Introduction of creating a 'learning environment' in which staff learn about their contribution to the success of the organization. To be successful, the employer and senior staff must be committed to the idea and offer the appropriate support and guidance to potential candidates. The quality assurance system as currently devised requires a great deal of paperwork and monitoring and care will have to be taken to ensure that the valuable aspects of the system are not dominated by paperwork. Although S/NVQs in general have been available for some ten years, it is still early days for ILS-S/NVQs. As more authorities start working with them and as more materials, such as the FastTrack materials, are published to support their use, many of the apprehensions currently being shown by some library authorities will start to diminish and this route will be accepted for its undoubted contribution to paraprofessional staff development and recognition.

References

1   Information and Library Services Lead Body, Information and library service scheme booklet, level 2, Coventry, RSA, 1996.
2   Hobson, J., 'The silent revolution at work', Library Association record, 98 (4), 1996, 202–3.
3   Pickles, N. and Totterdell, A., 'Towards a better workforce', Library Association record, 98 (2), 1996. 91, 93.
4   Hare, C., 'Forging a partnership with HE', Library Association record, 98 (9), 1996, 466–8.
5   Arundale, J., Getting your S/NVQ: a guide for candidates in the information and library sector, London, Library Association Publishing. Published in association with the Information and Library Services Lead Body, 1996.

6 Managing training

6.1 Factors affecting training management

In-house training, external training, educational provision and S/NVQs are all options open to library personnel but, as noted earlier, because staff training is crucially important for the development and continuing improvement of services, it requires effective, careful management. The major factor influencing the management of training in most organizations is the need for it to be seen as relevant not only to the organization but also to the individual. It is only through having a motivated and committed group of individuals working together that strong library assistant teams can be sustained.

Although the management implications of training within libraries will vary enormously depending on the size of the library and its organizational structure, it is possible to identify certain guiding principles. As with all other management functions, decisions about staff training and development will be influenced by the prevailing management style and nurturing a training culture will help to ensure that staff development remains uppermost in most employee's thoughts.

Training management involves four factors:

- responsibility for the training function
- identifying organizational and individual training needs
- responsibility for policies, resources and training mechanisms
- evaluation of training.

6.1.1 *Responsibility for the training function*

Formal responsibility for training must rest with the senior management of the library and their demonstrable attitudes towards the training function will determine how other supervisors and staff view training. The person charged with taking it forward must be sufficiently senior to ensure that policies are implemented. It will be incumbent upon the senior management to ensure that all managers and supervisors accept responsibility for their staff's training and development; central to this is the identification of opportunities and active encouragement of continuous improvement. This is a difficult and often thankless task and even organizations with the best of intentions need to make conscious efforts to keep training in the fore-front of everyone's minds.

Most libraries have a training officer or a senior member of staff desig-nated as responsible for training. Care must be taken to ensure that this role is clarified and understood by all. Is this person charged with carrying out training activities or merely coordinating activities suggested and orga-nized by other members of staff? Clearly the person in this role must have an overview of the library's development plans, staff interests and needs.

As a result s/he will need to be closely involved with identifying training needs and evaluating training. Perhaps his/her most important task will be instilling the training culture in all staff. Much of the success of this will depend on the personality and style of the job holder and how these traits match with the culture of the organization. It is also very important for this person to have a thorough understanding of learning theories and training methods so that external courses can be assessed for level and content before money is committed. These skills will also prove invaluable when preparing internal documentation and offering guidance on proposed approaches to individual staff training.

6.1.2   *Identifying training needs – organizational and individual*

For training to be relevant and effective, needs have to be identified and matched with appropriate training opportunities. This is particularly true in an era of diminishing resources. Within any organization someone must be charged with bringing that information together. Evidence from the new universities suggests that, where a training officer post exists, that post holder is responsible for compiling a training programme based on interviews conducted with professional staff, team leaders and supervisors.[1] Various methods of carrying out training needs analysis can be identified[2] and the method appropriate to the size of the library should be selected.

The training officer should be a senior staff member able to marry up individual requests with the library's overall strategic plan. There are frequently several sets of needs in operation within a large library environment: the individual, the library, the parent authority and the profession. There may be occasions when these competing needs cannot easily be reconciled and therefore staff must be kept informed of the reasons why it may not be possible for an individual request to be met. Although being coordinated by a senior member of staff it is essential that supervisors are fully appraised of overall policies and priorities so that library assistants have an easy point of contact to discuss their needs. Within large or dispersed libraries it may be necessary to establish a training committee composed of different grades of staff who can then be informed of organizational priorities. The contribution that library assistants can make to such committees should not be underestimated and the improved understanding of issues which permeates the library as a result is worthwhile.

The introduction of schemes such as career review has given every member of staff an opportunity to talk through development with his/her supervisor and therefore has put training and development on everyone's agenda. Problems which arise from this are associated with expectations not being met; whoever carries out the reviews needs to have a clear understanding of the library's objectives and the size of the training budget and work within these limits to ensure that staff expectations can be met. In such cases it is important for staff to remember that not all development necessarily involves training sessions.

Flexible workers
Any discussion of training priorities within libraries should encompass all categories of staff: it is easy to overlook the needs of an increasingly important category of staff – that of the 'flexible worker'. A flexible worker can be part-time, temporary and/or casual and many libraries now regard them as vital to maintenance of service provision. They may work few hours,

may not be available when training is taking place, or may leave at the end of their temporary contract. However, if we bear in mind the customer focus then such staff will be representing the library and therefore need access to training as much as, if not more than, full-time staff. The challenge for the training officer is to ensure access to training for this group of staff either through non-standard time training sessions or through the development of in-house training packages. Anne Goulding and Evelyn Kerslake[3] are currently funded by the British Library Research and Development Department to investigate this topic and it seems likely that the results of their research will influence future thinking on this aspect of training for library assistants.

Another factor which is regularly overlooked in relation to part-time staff is their lack of opportunity to practice their skills: a library assistant who works 12 hours a week, possibly during the evenings or weekends, will take at least three times as many weeks to acquire a week's work experience. Supervisors frequently fall into the trap of expecting too much from part-time staff who in some instances are not even given an adequate induction into the library service, its aims and ethos.

6.1.3 *Responsibility for policies, resources and training mechanisms*

Libraries should publish a training policy which clearly states their commitment to training and development. It may also encompass training priorities, access to resources and preferred mode of training. The value of this statement is that it clarifies who is responsible for training and for whom training is being provided. It will signal to all library staff where they fit into the scheme and how the training programme will be organized, and for the library it will signal clearly to the parent organization that effective management of human resources is being exercised in an overall effort to maintain or improve service quality without increasing resource provision.[4] The Policy Statement of Aston University[5] stresses that training is a 'continuous process [and] a shared responsibility' which should take place 'in a supportive environment'. It then goes on to identify roles and responsibilities. It is stated very clearly who will be responsible for integrating human resource strategy with overall library strategy. The statement continues by identifying the individual responsibilities which key personnel and the staff in general hold. Importantly, it also links the library's practice with the university's approach.

A major issue which faces library assistants in relation to training is the perceived imbalance between professional staff and library assistants. Professional staff regularly have the opportunity to attend two- or three-day conferences or training events away from the workplace whereas, partly because of the nature of their work, library assistant training tends to be more locally based. Some of these concerns can be overcome by having staff reporting back regularly on training or development events. This may be done informally at team meetings or it may be more formally done by writing a brief report. In either case the important issue to consider is the relevance of the session to the library as a whole. If this practice is carried out effectively then all staff can feel a sense of involvement and benefit from all training events undertaken by library staff.

Economic factors
Uppermost in most managers' minds will be economic factors. The emphasis on value for money pervades all activities undertaken within libraries.

In the field of training it can be difficult to assess as the impact may not be immediately visible but rather incremental. Certain cost-effective measures can be considered, including cooperative training, bringing an external consultant to the workplace to carry out training, making better use of existing resources (staff and otherwise) within the library, and making more effective use of self study materials so that senior staff time is used in a supportive way rather than a purely instructional one. The past few years has seen a rapid expansion in the numbers of consultants offering specialist training in such topics as customer care, dealing with aggression, time management or IT skills – issues relevant to all staff – and many libraries have preferred to bring a trainer to the staff in order to ensure maximum coverage.

It can be all too easy to overlook the resources which are available within a library's own staff complement and decide to send staff for training elsewhere. However, most larger library services have specialists within different departments and their skills should be considered. To illustrate this point it is worth considering the situation in a multicampus university which has increased its network of CD-ROM services. As a result many users now expect library assistants to know more about these services. In most cases this was an interest shared by the assistants themselves and they were happy to be involved in such training. An external course run by a consultant was identified as being at an appropriate level, cost and availability. However, within the same library there was a team of subject librarians who spent a large proportion of their working days training students in the use of these same products. Why not use that resource to train existing staff? In addition to the obvious cost saving it would have the benefit of allowing an exchange of information about the work of each group of staff which could make a valuable contribution to the way in which each carried out their work: a benefit that would not have accrued from attending an external course. Taking it one step further, if a library has staff with these skills, why not invite assistants from other local libraries to attend, thus ensuring that there is an exchange of experience across libraries as well as within a service? It is important that all staff realize that training is about giving and exchanging as well as taking.

Training is expensive in time expended and the subject librarians in this example may have felt that training was imposing too heavy a burden on their overall duties. From the managers' point of view there may also have been the problem of not being able to release enough staff at any one time to make the session viable. However, some libraries have experimented with the idea of creating self-instructional packages which can be used by assistants as part of a supervized training programme. A package, once created, can be used by different staff at times convenient to them and the service. It then releases the staff contact time to being more a tutorial session, in which individual specific issues are addressed. This will give assistants more confidence and control over their own training while ensuring that staff contact time is used to maximum benefit. It also opens the channels to a regular discussion about training needs and sessions between assistants and their immediate supervisors. Anything which improves this communication must be considered as meeting the general objectives of creating a 'learning environment'.

6.1.4 Evaluation of training

Closely linked with costs is value for money and the impact that training is having on the service. It is very difficult to measure the direct impact training has on an individual's performance. Any training undertaken should be assessed against the original objectives, which will normally arise from the identified needs. This can best be carried out by the trainee, in conjunction with the line manager or training officer. The impact of skills training should be readily identifiable as some new task should have been mastered. Attitude or interpersonal skills training may be more difficult to assess and may only become apparent following a period of observation or discussion. This process may need to take place over an extended period of time as the impact of some training will be to effect a change in overall outlook to work and users.

In addition to assessing the impact of training sessions, it is important to evaluate the actual training sessions as improvements may be suggested, especially if the training is internal. If external, an evaluation will allow the training officer to make a judgement about the value of sending staff on courses run by a particular organization.

It is often extremely difficult to measure the value that accrues from a particular course. If more users are dealt with more quickly and with fewer mistakes then a definite value can be seen; however library work is not like a production line and such simplistic approaches are not always appropriate. Therefore, in making such an assessment, an element of subjectivity may be required but the overriding priority in evaluating training must be to remain as objective as possible.

6.2 Other issues

Opportunities for staff mobility are becoming fewer with the result that many libraries now have very well trained, experienced staff. For library managers this can present both an advantage and a challenge because such staff will need to have their energies channelled to ensure that the quality of service remains high and fresh. One disadvantage of training (and it seems a heresy to say it) is that staff may be trained to a level beyond which they normally operate. Libraries should take care to ensure that training needs are confined to the stated job description and that development training is not offered in a manner which will ultimately create frustration. Focusing on organizational needs and a questioning approach to how work is carried out should ensure that well trained staff are encouraged to consider how to improve their approach to completing the elements of their jobs. In Chapter 4 reference was made to the blurring of responsibilities between professional and traditionally 'non-professional' posts and if this trend is to continue then gradings, salaries and career recognition for such post holders must follow. As this may directly threaten librarians' professional status it is an issue which must be addressed by everyone who works in library and information units. The introduction of S/NVQs and the transferability which they bring may give rise to more movement and subsequently increased satisfaction amongst library assistant grades.

A final word about the management of training for library assistants: all organizations, libraries included, are now caught up in constant change. New technologies, external pressures and wider remits all contribute to making 'the job' anything but static. For some, this constant change can seem threatening and unrelenting. Careful management is required if such challenges are to be met and overcome. This requires good communication and a clear understanding of where the organization is going and a reiteration of the value of each individual to the successful achievement of these aims.

References

1   Oldroyd, M., 'The role of the library staff development and training manager in the new universities', *British journal of academic librarianship*, **9** (3), 1994, 201–8.
2   Williamson, M., *Training needs analysis*, London, Library Association Publishing, 1993.
3   Goulding, A. and Kerslake, E., 'A firm commitment to a flexible future', *Library Association record*, **97** (11), 1995, 605–7.
4   Oldroyd, *ibid.*
5   Aston University Library and Information Services, Staff development and training policy statement. Wetherly, J., *Management of training and staff development*, London, Library Association Publishing, 1994.

7 Conclusions

Quality and value for money are major themes in all aspects of public and private service provision. There may be a temptation to reduce training budgets, especially for staff working in service rather than developmental roles. However, with the emphasis on enhanced customer satisfaction such cutbacks will be short-sighted: training for library assistants has probably never had such an important role in the provision of quality services.

To be effective, training policies and procedures must evolve directly from the library's strategic plan. The introduction of career review schemes and training needs analysis should ensure that library assistants have their training needs acknowledged by the organization. To meet these needs, a carefully managed training programme should be devised in which training achieved should be recorded and accredited.

The objectives of the training offered to meet the identified needs should be carefully considered to ensure that the product is well planned and presented. For this to occur, the training officer must be familiar with a wide range of delivery mechanisms, training opportunities and approaches.

As important as the content of training is the need for a supportive environment. All staff must feel they can approach management to discuss their work and development and this may require supervisors and managers to develop skills of coaching and counselling.

In all training or education undertaken there is a necessity to draw direct links between theory and practice, and the development of S/NVQs will allow accreditation to be given for work-based training and activities, while also incorporating the supporting knowledge and understanding.

S/NVQs will also place responsibility for self development firmly with the individual. Through discussion with the employer, the employee should be given opportunities to gain credit for work that is undertaken against a nationally recognized set of standards.

The more flexible approach offered by the introduction of S/NVQs should also cater for the needs of flexible workers by allowing credit to be gained outside the normal confines of established training and education sessions.

Libraries need to be training for quality and both employers and employees need to accept their responsibilities in ensuring that training occurs. All the approaches outlined in this volume have a part to play in the future development of library assistants that will lead to a recognized career structure for paraprofessionals.

Select bibliography

Adams, J., 'Customer care training in public libraries: do trainees perceive themselves to benefit?', *Public library journal*, **11** (2), 1996, 61–4.

Arundale, J., *Getting your S/NVQ: a guide for candidates in the information and library sector*, London, Library Association Publishing. Published in association with the Information and Library Services Lead Body, 1996.

Baker, D., 'Training and education of technicians and assistants in library work', *Library management*, **8** (6), 1987.

Blanksby, M., *Staff training: a librarian's handbook*, Newcastle under Lyme, AAL Publishing, 1988.

Bluck, R., *Team management*, London, Library Association Publishing, 1996.

Bryant, S. L., *Personal professional development and the solo librarian*, London, Library Association Publishing, 1995.

Corrall, S., 'Staff development: whose responsibility?', *Library manager*, **9** (July/August), 1995, 10–11.

Daniels, R. J., 'Effects on non-professional staff of the implementation of computer-based library systems in college libraries: some case studies', *Program*, **29** (1), 1995, 1–13.

Fairbrother, V., 'Co-operative training, open learning and public library staff', *Public library journal*, **9** (1), 1994, 10–14.

Herzog, J., *Implementing S/NVQs in the information and library sector: a guide for employers*, London, Library Association Publishing, 1996.

Hobson, J., 'The silent revolution at work', *Library Association record*, **98** (4), 1996, 202–3.

Lantz, B., 'Staff training for information technology', *British journal of academic librarianship*, **2** (1), 1987, 44–64.

Levy, P., *Interpersonal skills*, London, Library Association Publishing, 1993.

MacDougall, A. and Prytherch, R. (eds.), *Co-operative training in libraries*, Aldershot, Gower, 1989.

Mills, S., *Interpersonal skills training manual*, London, TFPL, 1993.

Oldroyd, M. (ed.), *Staff development in academic libraries: present practice and future challenges*, London, Library Association Publishing, 1996.

Pickles, N. and Totterdell, A., 'Towards a better workforce', *Library Association record*, **98** (2), 1996, 91–3.

Prytherch, R. (ed.), *Handbook of library training practice*, Aldershot, Gower, 1986.

Russell, N. J., 'Professional and non-professional in libraries: the need for a new relationship', *Journal of librarianship*, **17** (4), 1985, 293–310.

Stott, H., 'A quick guide to achieving information and library services NVQs', *Managing information*, **3** (3), 1996, 36–8.

Webb, J., 'The non-professional in the academic library: education for paraprofessionalism', *Personnel training and education*, **7** (2), 1990, 21–7.

Webb, S., 'Personal development', *Library and information assistant*, **5** (2), 1993, 3–19.

Williamson, M., *Training needs analysis*, London, Library Association Publishing, 1993.

Useful addresses

The Library Association
7 Ridgmount Street
London WC1E 7AE
Tel: 0171 636 7543
Fax: 0171 436 7218

Information and Library Services Lead Body
c/o 7 Ridgmount Street
London WC1E 7AE
Tel: 0171 255 2271
Fax: 0171 637 0126
World Wide Web page with details of ILS-NVQs:
http://www.ilsnvq.org.uk.ilsnvq/

RSA Examination Board
Westwood Way
Coventry
Warwickshire CV4 8HS
Tel: 01203 470033
Fax: 01203 468080

City and Guilds of London Institute
76 Portland Place
London W1N 4AA
Tel: 0171 278 2468
Fax: 0171 436 7630

Scottish Vocational Education Council (SCOTVEC)
Hanover House
24 Douglas Street
Glasgow G2 7NG
Tel: 0141 248 7900
Fax: 0141 242 2244

Association for the Education and Training of Library Assistants and
  Library Technicians
Chris M. Smith (Secretary)
45 Surrey Road
Seaford
Sussex BN25 2NR

Fast Track Associates Ltd
Fast Track House
68a Southgate
Sleaford
Lincolnshire NG34 7RL
Tel: 01529 414915
Fax: 01529 413144

Appendices

Examples of programmes or courses for library assistants.

1   Interpersonal skills activity

2   Training and Development Partnership, library assistants

3   Learning and reflection using learning logs

4   Mentoring scheme

5   EMALINK - aims and objectives of cooperative training group

6   Information and Library Services S/NVQ: Levels 2, 3 and 4

7   NVQ in Information and Library Services – Level 2, Unit 2

8   ILS NVQ Level 2 / C&G 737

9   College certificate course

ACTIVITY 1   WHAT IMAGE DO WE WANT TO CREATE?

OBJECTIVES   To determine and clarify the image we want to create for our users and visitors.

NUMBERS   Any size group.

TIME   Approx 1½ hrs.

RESOURCES   Document lA.
Document lB.
Flip chart, stand, large pens.

VIDEO   Scene 1, 2, 8, 9.

METHOD	*TRAINER'S GUIDE*
1. Introduce the activity by stating the objectives.	You may wish to emphasise the following points: a) Visitors will react to our mistakes and remember them. Word gets round. b) Visitors will react to any rudeness or impatience and will not look for any reasons to excuse it. c) Visitors will notice untidy appearance. d) Our image is the responsibility of all staff members and must be consistent. e) A good image raises our profile and hence makes our jobs easier and more enjoyable.

Allow 10 minutes for this part of the exercise.

2. Ask the group to suggest examples of shops or other organisations that have worked hard to promote a good image. Encourage each participant to relate their good/bad experiences and explain what impressed/dismayed them.	a) How effective are they at producing a good image? b) How does a 'good image organisation' affect how you behave to its personnel? c) How does a 'poor image organisation' affect your behaviour and approach?

Allow 15 minutes for this part of the exercise.

3.   Issue Document lA to the participants.
Divide the group into 2's, 3's or 4's (depending on the size of the group).

Appendix 1 continued

4. Ask each group to place, in each circle, what they believe are the main 'image making' issues to which all staff can apply themselves.	Encourage participants to think about the 'whole image'. What should be the first impressions of the environment? What should be the impressions visitors get of us? Consider what we say, how we say it, how we greet people, what we look like, how we receive their problems and how we deal with difficult problems. How efficient and well organised are we?

Allow 30 minutes for this part of the exercise.

5. Plenary session. Ask each group to elect a spokesperson. Using the flip chart, record the 'image making issues' that have been raised in each group. Condense these issues into 4 main areas and re-write them on the flip chart.	a) What issues constantly appear? b) How good are we NOW? c) What could we improve? d) Should we be considering changes in any areas in order to help staff members?

Allow 15 minutes for this part of the exercise.

6. Issue Document 1B.
   Ask each participant to write a
   maximum of 4 areas that they could
   work on to assist in creating the
   right image.
   Transfer the 4 main areas
   for departmental attention onto
   Document 1B.

Allow 5 minutes for this part of the exercise.

7. Ask each participant to discuss with their partner or group the 4 areas for personal attention.	a) Ask your group to explain why they have selected these issues. b) Can you help this person by suggesting ideas and giving advice on any of the issues.

Allow 10 minutes for this part of the exercise.

Appendix 1 .continued

8. End the activity by highlighting the main points that have been mentioned and how each person can take 'ownership' of departmental image but how they may, in return, expect assistance from colleagues and departmental heads.	Suggest that the group consider Document 1B in 2 months' time to discuss progress and obstacles for themselves and their departments.

DOCUMENT 1A

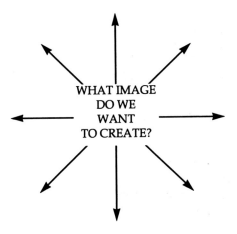

DOCUMENT 1B

AREAS FOR ME TO WORK ON

1 ....

2 ....

3 ....

4 ....

AREAS FOR THE DEPARTMENT TO WORK ON

1 ....

2 ....

3 ....

4 ....

Source: Mills, S., *Interpersonal skills training manual*, London, TFPL, 1993.

Appendix 2 Training and Development Partnership, library assistants

LIBRARIES AND HERITAGE DIVISION

The aims of the Leisure Services Department are to recognise the value of people in the provision of leisure services, and to provide services that are responsive to the needs of the community.

In order to achieve these aims, the Leisure Services Dept. will work in partnership with all employees to enable them to reach their full potential through training, development and education, so that they can contribute fully to the success of the department.

Who is responsible for your development?

YOU
by:
* accepting responsibility for your own development
* exploring your abilities and making full use of them
* understanding your strengths and identifying areas for improvement
* discussing your needs and goals with your manager
* continuing to learn
* taking opportunities when they arise

YOUR MANAGER
by:
* giving guidance and support
* stretching your abilities
* finding opportunities for your training and development
* evaluating and giving feedback

THE LEISURE SERVICES DEPARTMENT
by:
* providing an environment which encourages training and development
* offering and creating opportunities for growth
* providing the necessary training for your job
* making clear the skills it values

What are the benefits?

FOR YOU:
* increased job satisfaction and effectiveness
* confidence in your own abilities
* the skills you need now and in the future
* opportunities to develop

FOR YOUR MANAGER:
* satisfaction from seeing people grow
* highly competent staff who get results

FOR THE LEISURE SERVICES DEPARTMENT:
* employees with the skills needed to provide a quality service
* the right people at the right time to meet and be responsive to needs
* leadership continuity
* improved performance and productivity
* a committed and skilled workforce

Appendix 2 continued

How can you develop your skills?

You need to have clear objectives about what you need to learn and how to make best use of the skills gained. For this reason, certain *Core Competencies* have been identified for Library Assistants and Senior Library Assistants within the Libraries and Heritage Division along with the training options/opportunities available for each.

Make use of this list when preparing for your planning appraisal in September and make sure that you and your line manager identify the training needed to develop your full potential.

Remember that the list is neither prescriptive nor exhaustive and that *your* ideas are an integral part of the partnership.

Your manager will of course also identify any new service developments or specific initiatives which are scheduled to take place and which require special training; this will be incorporated into your training plan.

PLEASE!!! Give yourself some time before your planning appraisal to think about your needs and ask yourself if there is anything you need to know or understand, or be able to do in order to improve your performance, your career prospects or service delivery. You can then discuss with your line manger what *you* hope to achieve and how it will benefit you, the service and ultimately the customer. Your manager may also have some ideas about your training and development which will also be incorporated into your training plan.

Should any additional training needs become apparent through the year (either to you, your manager, the Division or the Department), these will of course be addressed and the training plan revised.

Our success depends on the skills and abilities of the Division's employees. The continuing development of all employees is therefore a key responsibility for everyone involved in the partnership.

LIBRARY ASSISTANTS

The success of the Libraries and Heritage Division depends on the skills and abilities of its employees.

Whilst operational skills are vital to doing the job, Libraries and Heritage recognises that there are other skills which are essential to the provision of a quality service to the customer.

As you think about your annual planning appraisal, use the following to help you decide what training and development activities would benefit you. Your line manager will have further ideas which will be incorporated into your training plan.

Because of the different nature of the work, a separate list has been produced for library assistants in Bibliographical Services. However, certain elements here may still be appropriate.

CORE COMPETENCE	*TRAINING/METHOD OPTIONS*
1. *Basic skills*	
Library operations/procedures	O, OJ, SLA
Administrative procedures	P, SLA
Reservation procedures	B, CL, O, OJ, SLA
Operate computerised and non~computerised libs	O, OJ, SLA
Know how books are selected and ordered	B, CL
Office Power	SLA, T24

Appendix 2 continued

2. *Service specific*
   Reference and enquiry services:
   knowledge of Central Ref .... A, S, T6
   handling enquiries .... CL, R, T6
   know your library's stock & other sources of info. CL, R, T6

   Community Care services:
   knowledge of the section .... A
   services to specific groups .... A, CVI, T5
   disabilities awareness .... A, CVI, T5

   Museums service: .... A, S

   Local Studies .... A, Si T4

   Services to children and young people:
   School Library Service .... A, PL
   assist in children's activities/events .... CL, T1
   assist with class visits CL
   know about the stock .... CL, T8
   demonstrate and use CD-ROMs (at relevant libs) CL, SLA

   Open Learning (at relevant libs) .... CL, T3

   Ethnic minorities .... A

   Bibliographical Services .... B

   Publicity and promotion .... E

3. *Communication skills*
   Good oral and written communication ...... OL, SLA, T17
   Confident and friendly telephone manner ... OJ, OL, SLA, T17

4. *Personal skills*
   Handle difficult customers and complaints ... T18, TT23
   Be helpful to colleagues and customers T17
   Work as part of a team T17
   Make your point clearly, reasonably and assertively OL, T17, TT30/31
   Present a positive personal image to customers OL, T17, TT5

5. *Personal effectiveness*
   Understand the impact of your work T117, TT2000
   Plan and organise events/activities T1
   Have ideas to improve quality .... CI, T22
   Understand the organisation .... A, BP, TT2000
   Understand basic supervisory techniques ... OL, T15, TT33

6. *Health and safety/staff welfare*
   Maintain a safe environment .... OJ, OL, P, SLA, TT29
   Use and control of hazardous substances ... OJ, P, SLA, TT28
   Deal with accidents and incidents .... OJ, P, SLA, T17, T18
   Lift and handle goods safely .... P, SLA, TT24
   Plan for retirement TT8
   First Aid TT25/26/27

KEY TO ABBREVIATIONS

A	Awareness package available from relevant Section Head
AS	Training/experience provided by Area Supervisor
B	bib. site visit
BP	Business Plan
CI	Continual Improvement projects
CL	Training/experience provided by Community Librarian
CVI	CVI site visit
E	External training course
G	printed guidelines
O	Operational Manual
OJ	On-job training checklist
OL	Open Learning pack (see Appendix 3)
P	procedural Manual
PL	Project Loans secondment
R	Reference service practice notes (including monthly updates)
S	Site visit
SLA	Training/experience provided by SLA
T	L&H training course (subject to demand - see Appendix 1)
TT	Tameside Training course *may be* available (see Appendix 2)
TT2000	Tameside Towards 2000 manual

LIBRARY ASSISTANTS - BIBLIOGRAPHICAL SERVICES

CORE COMPETENCES:

1   Telephone procedures
    Induction/in-house course

2   Customer care
    Induction/course

3   Health and Safety procedures including COSHH etc.
    Induction/on-going training

4   Lifting and handling procedures Course

5   Circulation procedures:
    Checkin/checkout
    Place a hold
    Inquiry: Patron
    Inquiry: Show Search
    inquiry: Title
    In post: workplace training

6   Book Acquisitions procedures:
    Order
    Receipt
    POINQUIRY
    TITLEQUERY
    Search
    Physical processing
    In post: workplace training

Appendix 2 continued

7   CLCAT searching
     In post: workplace training

8   Request and interlending procedures
     In post: workplace training

9   Use of the UNITY database
     Course/In post: workplace training

10   Collection of data
     In post: workplace training

11   Use of RED CD-Rom
     In post: workplace training

12   Use of BOOKBANK CD-Rom
     In post: workplace training

13   Use of supplier's CD-Rom selection tools
     In post: workplace training

14   Approvals: unpacking and checking etc.
     In post: workplace training

15   Teachers' Centre procedures
     In post: workplace training

APPENDIX 1

LIBRARIES AND HERITAGE DIVISION TRAINING COURSES

The following is a list of in-house courses which may be available, subject to demand.
PLEASE NOTE: these courses can be tailored to meet particular needs but you must
identify these when the course is requested.

COURSE	DURATION
SERVICE SPECIFIC:	
T1 Children's activities	1 day
T2 National Curriculum	½ day
T3 Open Learning (for relevant libraries)	as needed
T4 Local Studies	1 day
T5 Disability awareness	1 day
T6 Reference and enquiry work	1 day
T7 Database searching	1 day
STOCK:	
T8 Junior stock and selection	1 day
T9 Adult book selection	1 day
TI0 Book trade/book supply	1 day
T11 Unity database	Bib demo on request
T12 CD-ROM bibliographies	Bib demo on request

Appendix 2 continued

MANAGEMENT DEVELOPMENT:	
T13 Managing meetings	½ day
T14 Employment legislation	½ day
T15 Supervisory skills	1 day
T16 Time management/work planning	1 day
PERSONAL SKILLS:	
T17 Customer care	1 day
T18 Dealing with difficult customers	½ day
T19 Handling the media	½ day
MISCELLANEOUS:	
T20 Energy conservation	½ day
T21 Tameside Towards 2000	½ day
T22 Continual Improvement awareness	½ day
T23 Appraisal planning and conducting	½ day
T24 Office Power: introduction	½ day

APPENDIX 2

TRAINING COURSES AVAILABLE FROM CENTRAL PERSONNEL/IT DEPT.

These have all been run during 1995, however most are subject to demand. Those which have been run on a regular basis are marked with an asterisk (*).

COURSE	DURATION
MANAGING PEOPLE:	
TT1 An introduction to Counselling skills *	2 days
TT2 Motivating and empowering employees *	2 days
SERVING THE PUBLIC:	
TT3 Improving the quality of your service	1 day
TT4 Marketing your service for competition	1½ days
TT5 Customer Care	I day
DEVELOPING YOURSELF, DEVELOPING YOUR STAFF:	
TT6 Management development NVQ 3/4	36 half days
TT7 Leadership for change	1 day
TT8 Pre-retirement	2 days
TT9 Introduction to management	4 days (over 4 weeks)
TT10 Train the trainer	2 days (over 2 weeks)
TT11 Team building	2 days
TT12 Team leadership	2 days
THE EMPLOYMENT RELATIONSHIP:	
TT13 Managing absence *	1 day
TT14 Recruitment and selection *	2 days
TT15 Hearing employee grievances	2 days
TTI6 Dealing with disciplinary interviews	2 days
TT17 Handling conflict/difficult staff issues	2 days

Appendix 2 continued

GETTING WORK DONE:
TT18 Managing your time *	2 days (over 2 weeks)
TT19 Project management *	3 days + review day
TT20 Employee resource planning	1 day

CREATING A POSITIVE WORK CULTURE:
TT21 Helping you to manage your stress *	1 day
TT22 Stress awareness for managers	1 day
TT23 Dealing with violence and aggression at work *	1½ days
TT24 Manual handling and lifting	I day
TT25 Basic First Aid	1 day
TT26 First Aid at work	4 days
TT27 First Aid at work (refresher)	1 day
TT28 COSHH/AIDS awareness	½ day
TT29 Health and Safety general awareness	1 day

EQUALITY IN THE WORKPLACE:
TT30 Assertiveness for women *	2 days
TT31 Assertiveness for men *	1 day
TT32 Managing incidents of harassment at work	1 day
TT33 Women into management Part 1	2 days
TT34 Women into management Part 2	2 days
TT35 Dealing with survivors of domestic violence	½ days
TT36 Women returners	1 day
TT37 Supporting employees who face harassment - (training for departmental contacts)	1 day

THE DEMOCRATIC PROCESS:
TT38 Welcome to Tameside	1 day
TT39 Public presentations *	2 days
TT40 Delegation - the art of letting go	1 day
TT41 Communicating by letter *	1 day
TT42 Writing a good report *	1 day
TT43 Managing meetings	1 day

IT SKILLS:
TT44 Office Power overview *	1 day
TT45 Introduction to Windows *	1 day
TT46 Introduction to word processing	½ day
TT47 Office Power word processing - basic *	2 days
TT48 Office Power word processing - advanced	1 day

APPENDIX 3

Open learning packages

The Open Learning Centre at Hyde (and Central from September 1996) contains a wide selection of training packages all relating to job skills. The attached list gives a selection of what is available which *may help* to address certain identified training needs of L&H staff. Managers and supervisors are welcome to visit the centre(s) to examine the stock and borrow suitable material for use on site with staff.

Appendix 2 continued

TITLE	FORMAT	SUBJECT
How to be assertive	T	A
Managing information: writing skills	A, T	C
Effective business writing: a self learning guide	T	C
Assertive communication skills for professionals	T, V	C
How to write reports	T	C
The art of communicating: achieving interpersonal impact in business	T	C
The business of listening: a practical guide to effective listening	T	C
Writing letters: how to write letters that work for you	T	C
Counselling listener	A, T	Co
Counselling skills	A, T	Co
Empowering employees through delegation	T	D
Leadership: the art of delegation	T	D
Managing human resources: delegation	A, T	D
Management products and services: health and safety	A, T	HS
Management and leadership skills for women	A	M
Management products and services: ensuring quality	A, T	M
Moving into management: a course for women	A, T V	M
Mastering change	T, V	M
Managing human resources: team leading	A, T	M
Managing human resources: leading change	A, T	M
Managing information: meetings	A, T	M
Influencing others: a handbook of persuasive strategies	T	M
Effective presentation skills: a practical guide for better speaking	T	P
Making presentations	A, T, V	P
Managing information: speaking skills	A, T	P
Self-esteem for women	A, T	P
Managing stress	A, T, V	S
Managing stress for mental fitness	T	S
Stress management for professionals: staying balanced under pressure. Video workbook	T	S
Stress management for professionals: staying balanced under pressure. Volume 1	V	S
Stress management for professionals: staying balanced under pressure. Volume 2	V	S
Stress management for professionals: staying balanced under pressure. Volume 3	V	S
First-time supervisor's survival guide	T	SM
Managing human resources: supervising at work	A, T	SM
Managing human resources: supervising with authority	A, T	SM
Managing people	T	SM
Professional supervision skills	A, T	SM
Supervisory management: principles and practice	T	SM
The first time supervisor	T	SM
The new supervisor: skills for success	T	SM
Management of time	T, V	T
Managing time	T, V	T
Managing your time	T	T
Taking control of your work day	T, V	T
Time management	T	T

Appendix 2 continued

KEY TO ABBREVIATIONS USED:

Format:	A	Audio cassette(s)
	T	Text based material (books, leaflets, worksheets etc.)
	V	Video(s)
Subject:	A	Assertiveness
	C	Communication - written and oral
	Co	Counselling
	O	Delegation
	NS	Health and Safety
	M	Management skills
	P	presentation skills
	S	Stress management
	SM	Supervisory management
	T	Time management

Source: Tameside Metropolitan Borough, Tameside Leisure Services. Libraries and Heritage, Library Assistant Training & Development.

Appendix 3 Learning and reflection using logos

NAPIER UNIVERSITY STAFF DEVELOPMENT
MENTORING SCHEME

"Learning and Reflection"

Learning logs or diaries can play a useful part in developing a deeper level of reflection. Keeping a diary makes learning from experience a more deliberate and conscious process rather than accidental. Else (1992) suggests that there are advantages of *consciously* learning from experience:

"It helps you to learn from your successes, not just from your mistakes.

It makes it more likely that you will transfer your learning.

It can help you to plan for future, similar situations; to plan what you will do the same, what you will do differently."

New members of staff should experiment with keeping logs which relate to their development objectives. For example, a "Stress Log" of situations or people who cause higher stress levels, a "Time Management Diary" listing time spent in relation to priority tasks, a "Critical Incidents Log" with descriptions of significant positive and negative incidents over a period of time. The possibilities are almost endless since the "log" can focus on a specific project or skill or encompass the whole job. In any case, the key questions are basically the same:

- WHAT HAPPENED? (description of the situation, event, etc...)
- HOW DID I FEEL? (description of the learners' emotional reaction to the situation)
- WHAT DID I DO? (description of actions taken and why)
- WHAT COULD I HAVE DONE DIFFERENTLY? (description of alternative courses of action)
- SO, WHAT NOW? (what are the implications for what I think, feel, do in the future).

Appendix 3 continued

**NAPIER UNIVERSITY STAFF DEVELOPMENT
MENTORING SCHEME**

"Learning Log"

Name: ....

Area of Development: ....

Date: ....

WHAT HAPPENED?

HOW DID I FEEL?

WHAT DID I DO?

WHAT COULD I HAVE DONE DIFFERENTLY?

SO, WHAT NOW?

Appendix 4 Mentoring scheme

NAPIER UNIVERSITY STAFF DEVELOPMENT
MENTORING SCHEME

"What is Mentoring"

The definition of a mentor given by Clutterbuck (1992) is a useful starting point: *"A mentor is a more experienced individual, willing to share his/her knowledge with someone less experienced in a relationship of mutual trust"*.

Clutterbuck goes on to describe the key roles of mentoring as:

- COACH: developing the skills of the mentee through constructive feedback and guidance.
- COUNSELLOR: acting as a sounding board.
- FACILITATOR: smoothing the path of the mentee.
- NETWORKER: showing the mentee how to get things done outwith the formal organisational structures.

An alternative description of the mentor's role is offered by Tuck (1993): *"The mentor has several functions in helping learners to reflect on such experiences as they are acquired:*

- *as an enabler of the self-assessment process;*
- *as a 'mirror' to the learners' own ambitions and understandings;*
- *as a provider of 'unconditional positive regard'."*

In individual cases, the role of the mentor will depend on a number of factors:

- the needs and expectations of the person being mentored;
- the knowledge, experience and development style of the mentor;
- the learning and development objectives defined by the University and Department.

These issues must be fully explored at an early stage in any mentoring relationship and should be revisited as they will inevitably change over time.

"Examples of Good Practice"

- Having a mutually agreed mentoring contract
- Planning a series of one-to-one meetings into your diary
- Keeping a brief record of mentoring meetings and discussions
- Use electronic mail to complement other communications
- Actively listen, don't dictate
- Show you are human by talking about yourself and your interests
- Playing 'devil's advocate'
- Arranging visits outwith the workplace
- Giving responsibility to the mentee
- Working with the mentee on a project
- Continually review progress and revise learning objectives.

"Examples of Poor Practice"

- Missing scheduled meetings
- Being unavailable
- Making no effort to find useful information/contacts. Giving vague, unspecific feedback
- Rushing meetings
- Meeting in a busy office
- Discussing your problems more than theirs
- Passing on information about the mentoring relationship without permission.

Adapted from: Mentoring Handbook, University of Glamorgan

"Coaching Skills"

New members of staff who are at an early stage in their career, or who have recently changed career, may particularly want their mentor to coach them in their new role. Coaching is a supportive development process which helps individuals set and achieve challenging goals as preparation for the future. Kalinauckas and King (1994) state: *"For coaching to be fully effective, there has to be an adult to adult relationship between the coach and the person being coached. It is about developing productive working relationships, not controlling people like children."*

Coaching involves a number of key skills:

- Active Listening — encourage the mentee to give their input, allow silences.
- Questioning — open, probing questions which encourage reflection and learning (see below for examples).
- Giving Praise — give recognition for achievements, build confidence through positive feedback.
- Gaining Trust — need to build trust by developing a rapport, being supportive and non-judgemental.
- Observation — picking up on visual clues such as body language.
- Action-orientated — although discussions can be wide-ranging, expanding the individual's critical thinking, it is important to focus on achievable outcomes which will be followed through.

Coaching Questions

What do you want to achieve?
How do you see yourself doing that?
What resources will you need?
Who else do you need to work with?
Do you have alternative options?
What will completion look like?
How could you do better next time?
What evidence do you have for your viewpoint?

Appendix 5   EMALINK – aims and objectives of cooperative training group

MEMBERS

De Montfort University, Derby University, Leicester University, Loughborough University, Nottingham Trent University, Nottingham University

AIMS

To exchange information on and share good practice in strategic human resource management in university library and information services;

To encourage and facilitate closer contact and communication between the staff of the six university library and information services;

To provide a mechanism for the promotion and organisation of cooperative training and staff development activities.

OBJECTIVES

The group's primary objectives are to:

– exchange information on HRM practice;

– arrange shared development and training activities including a termly programme of events;

– facilitate staff exchanges and visits;

– disseminate relevant research results and working documents;

– liaise, as appropriate, with other bodies e.g. EMBLA, UCRG, UCoSDA, M1/M69 Link.

STEERING GROUP

The Steering Group has 6 members – one from each of the participating universities. Each has responsibility for strategic human resource management issues (e.g. recruitment, appraisal, job evaluation, staff development) and is necessarily, therefore, at deputy/second tier management level.
Since a number of other staff are now involved in the operational management of staff training activities, it has been agreed to hold one Steering Group meeting per annum, prior to the start of the financial/academic year, (the Group meets termly) to which these staff will also be invited. The specific purpose of that meeting will be to discuss the outcomes of the annual training needs analysis, possible content of the training events programme for the coming year and to provide an opportunity for exchange of experience in the peer group.

COMMITMENT

Each university in turn hosts the Steering Group meeting. Most EMALINK events are based on exchange of experience and expertise and they are free of charge. Each university also, therefore, commits itself to hosting and facilitating its fair share of events thus providing a cost-effective training medium for all.

Margaret Oldroyd (DMU representative) for the Steering Group 11/1995

| Appendix 6 | Information and Library Services S/NVQ: Levels 2, 3 and 4 |

Level 2
Candidates must complete all mandatory units and any three optional units, making a total of six units to gain the full qualification.

Mandatory Units
1   Process material for use
    All the basic skills in looking after the physical material which the library/information service holds
2   Identify and provide information/material required by user
    Basic assistance to users in locating and providing
3   Develop positive working relationships with customers
    Identifying and satisfying customers' needs - balancing these with the organisation's resources, and presenting a positive personal image

Optional Units
4   Maintain arrangement of information/material
    The tidy organisation of material to enable effective retrieval
5   Secure information/material
    Basic skills in maintaining security in a library/information unit. More appropriate for staff in larger organisations
6   Contribute to the maintenance of a supportive environment for users
    Basic work with users, covering routine maintenance of the physical environment, and a supervised role in taking user feedback and dealing with disruption
7   Direct users
    Provision of basic geographical guidance around the library/information unit, covering responsibility for providing written signs and verbal assistance. Appropriate for units where a self-service facility exists.
8   Issue & recover loan material
    All the basic circulation functions, including requisite customer care aspects. Appropriate for units which lend material
9   Maintain data in a computer system
    Ability to use a computer system to input, manipulate and retrieve data. Includes ability to use appropriate software, including the production and printing of documents in various forms

Level 3
Candidates must complete all mandatory units, one unit from each optional Group plus a further 2 units, making a total of nine units to gain the full qualification.

Mandatory Units
1   Provide information/material to user
    Use of inter-library loans and other reciprocal arrangements, as well as practical search and retrieval skills
2   Organise information/material
    Covers the traditional library functions of classification and cataloguing in traditional or non-traditional ways
3   Solve problems on behalf of customers
    Identifying the problem, solving it within the alternative solutions available, and referring elsewhere as appropriate
4   Maintain services & operations to meet quality standards
    Planning & organising, communicating clearly, ensuring quality standards, handling disruptions and recommending improvements

Appendix 6 continued

Optional Units : User Services

5   Identify information required by user
    *Covers "reference interviewing" to identify what specific information/material user requires.
    It involves sustained interaction with the user although this need not be face-to face*

6   Provide displays
    Covers the creation, maintenance and dismantling of a simple information display

7   Maintain a supportive environment for users
    *For staff who have direct responsibility for work with users. Includes overseeing the
    maintenance of the physical environment; and direct responsibility for dealing with user
    feedback and disruption*

8   Initiate and evaluate change to improve service to customers
    *Covers obtaining and handling feedback from customers, plus initiating and evaluating
    improvements to services*

Optional Units : Information Technology and Processing

9   Create new information/material
    *Provision & evaluation of current awareness services, listings services & other types
    of basic information*

10   Store and display information/material
    Storage and display of information/material

11   Maintain the IT solution
    *Basic equipment maintenance, creation of file structures and maintenance of media &
    documentation storage*

12   Produce numerical models using the IT solution
    *Entering, processing & outputting of numerical models, including manipulating models &
    graphs*

13   Produce documents using the IT solution
    *Entering, processing and outputting of documents, including manipulating text, numbers &
    graphics*

14   Communicate electronically using the IT solution
    Transmitting, receiving & accessing data electronically

Optional Units: Supervising Activities

15   Contribute to the planning, monitoring & control of resources
    *Includes making suggestions for improvements, communicating with others, keeping records,
    solving problems*

16   Contribute to the provision of personnel
    *Planning how to use staff, assess staff and select staff including legal requirements, record
    keeping and communicating*

17   Contribute to the training & development of teams, individuals and self to enhance
    performance
    *Planning training & development, assessing skills, setting objectives and motivating staff
    plus self-improvement in the job*

18   Contribute to the planning, organisation and evaluation of work
    *Reviewing work & suggesting improvements, building teams, discussing performance,
    decision-making & planning resources*

19   Create, maintain and enhance productive working relationships
    *Communicating & building relationships with staff, dealing with conflict, giving advice and
    making proposals for action*

Level 4
Candidates must complete all Mandatory units, plus one from each Option Group, plus two others, making a total of twelve units to gain the full qualification.

Mandatory Units
1 Identify strategy to meet user's complex information needs
   'Reference interviewing' to identify the area of information in which a user is interested, together with its scope and characteristics
2 Meet user's information needs
   Includes evaluation of information by selecting and highlighting for the user. The outcome here will not be a single item of information
3 Determine information/material requirements
   Covers the periodic review of needs and resources. The results of this activity may be fed into the process of reviewing selection policy
4 Plan storage and display
   Implementing or reviewing a new storage and display system.

Optional Units : User Services
7 Provide user education
   Designing and delivering specific learning programmes to help users get what they want from the organisation
8 Mount promotional event
   Deals with all the junctions in organising and revising an event
9 Design training and development sessions
   The design of training for individuals and groups, including selection of delivery methods
10 Facilitate learning in groups through presentations and activities
   Making effective formal and informal presentations, facilitating a range of structured activities or exercises
11 Support and advise individual learners
   Assisting learners in planning and managing their own learning, helping them to develop relevant skills, and ensuring support

Optional Units: Collection Management
12 Select information/material for acquisition
   The selection of new information/material within a selection policy
13 Acquire information/material
   The acquisition of information/material
14 Withdraw unwanted information/material
   The withdrawal of information/material

Optional Group: Specialist Information Activities
15 Undertake research project
   A specific research project, not necessarily academic in nature, within the information and library unit
16 Index information
   Covers "back of the book" indexing as well as the creation of a stand alone index of information.
17 Abstract information.
   The whole process of abstracting

Appendix 6 continued

Optional Units: Management
18 Recommend, monitor and control the use of resources
19 Contribute to the recruitment and selection of personnel
20 Develop teams, individuals and self to enhance performance
21 Plan, allocate and evaluate work carried out by teams, individuals & self
22 Create, maintain and enhance effective working relationships
23 Seek, evaluate and organise information for action
24 Exchange information to solve problems and make decisions

Information and Library Services Lead Body
c/o 7 Ridgmount Street
London WC1E 7AE
Tel: 0171 255 2271 Fax: 0171 637 0126
a.frampton@bbcnc.org.uk
http://www.ilsnvq.org.uk/ilsnvq/

NVQ in Information and Library Services – Level 2. Unit 2

UNIT 2: IDENTIFY AND PROVIDE INFORMATION/MATERIAL REQUIRED BY USER

Element 2.2: Identify availability of information/material

Performance Criteria
1 Search is effective and efficient, and capable of quick delivery
2 Appropriate information sources are selected
3 Any failure to locate exact requirements of user is clearly explained and alternatives offered where appropriate
4 All contact with the user is courteous and effective and user satisfaction is verified appropriately.

Range
1 **Information sources**: catalogue of own information/material, external providers
2 **Failure due to**: non-existence of information, beyond scope of organisation, information lost
3 **Alternatives**: photocopy, microform, material on similar topic, faxed copy, referral to more appropriate source.

Knowledge
All performance criteria:
• What information and sources are available
PC 2:
• Sufficient subject knowledge to identify appropriate sources.

In all cases, supplementary evidence may be provided to support demonstration of the underpinning knowledge and understanding through competent performance.

Guidance
Performance evidence:
• Work products, i.e. written notes, file notes, search records, letters/reports
• Observation
• Personal report of actual work situation/s
• Witness reports, from colleagues and/or users
Supplementary evidence:
• Questioning, in areas of the range where no performance evidence is provided
• Verbal/written tests of knowledge and understanding, where this cannot be demonstrated through performance evidence.

Appendix 7 continued

Evidence Specifications

Sufficiency of evidence:
- Items in the range for which performance evidence must be provided: both from **1**, one from **2**, one from **3**
- All other aspects of the range must be covered, either by performance evidence or supplementary evidence
- Candidates should be able to demonstrate consistency of performance over a period time, and can use supplementary evidence to do so.

Currency of evidence:
- Where evidence for this element has been achieved more than three years before the date of assessment, the candidate will be expected to provide supplementary evidence to show that s/he can transfer competent performance to a current context.

Context of evidence:
- Specially generated performance evidence, from assignments/projects or temporary transfer to a new working environment, may be needed for the candidate to demonstrate competence. Exceptionally, a scenario may be simulated to provide support to performance evidence generated from naturally occurring performance at work.

Appendix 8 ILS NVQ level 2 / C&G 737

Library and Information Assistants' Certificate
National Vocational qualifications (NVQs) in Library and Information work have now been introduced and students will be entered at level 2 in conjunction with the practical elements of City and Guilds 737, thus giving them the opportunity to achieve the formal practical competences of NVQ as well as the more theoretically based City and Guilds Library' and Information Assistants' Certificate in one course

Course content
The NVQ 2 comprises six units: (i–iii compulsory + 3 others)
i   Process material for use
ii   Identify and provide information/material required by user
iii   Develop positive working relationships with customers
iv   Maintain arrangement of material
v   Secure information/material
vi   Contribute to the maintenance of a supportive environment for users
vii   Direct users
viii   Issue and recover loan material
ix   Maintain data in a computer system

The City and Guilds course is currently being revised, and will consist of 4 units of competence covering the main area of para-professional library and information work

Education and Career Opportunities
This course provides the theoretical background and the practical competence training necessary for the efficient and informed practice of a wide range of jobs within the library and information sector, enhancing confidence in existing roles and providing opportunities for career progression.

Methods of Study
There are several options:
a   Weekly attendance at college 1.00–4.30 on Tuesdays, either September to May, or January to December
b   Semi-distance route, involving one day per month at college (a Wednesday 9.30–4.30) with the rest of the course in distance learning packages for home study (approximately 4–5 hours per week) commencing either September or January
c   Full distance learning route – two formats:
      with all material in distance learning format, supported by telephone contact with tutor;
      with all material in distance learning format, the student will receive a FAX machine for the duration of the course, and contact with the tutor will be by fax or by telephone when necessary.
      Entry either September or January
d   Short course route – a twelve-week course, running each week from February to May, and involving three days' college attendance, one day's work experience, arranged by the college, and one study day. There are two study weeks for this route, and ten teaching weeks making the total course twelve weeks. This route will only run if sufficient students are interested.

For whom the course is intended
Candidates on routes a–c should normally be currently employed in a library or information unit, though this can be arranged by the college where necessary on a part time or voluntary basis.

Entry requirements
4 GCSEs at grade C or above, or equivalent.

Duration
All routes except the twelve-week short course run from September to May or from January to December.

Qualifications and methods of assessment
ILS NVQ 2 and a City and Guilds Certificate, which are nationally recognised qualifications for library and information assistants, will be awarded to each candidate who passes. ILS/NVQ2 is assessed in a workplace context to externally verified standards. City and Guilds 737 has four externally marked theoretical examinations, and four practical assessments undertaken in a workplace context and assessed to externally verified standards.

Application and further details
Please contact: Anne Totterdell, Library Education Tutor on 01823 366448.

Appendix 9 College certificate course

Supervisory skills for Senior Library and Information Assistants

Course content
The eight sessions will cover the following areas:
What is Management?
Staffing structures
Working in teams
Dealing with conflict
Dealing with change
Personal effectiveness
Delegation
Time management
The special features of library management
Planning.

Education and Career Opportunities
This course aims to consolidate the exercise of a range of skills in senior para-professional staff already fulfilling supervisory roles, thus increasing expertise and confidence in existing roles, and to introduce these skills to staff who feel ready to undertake supervisory roles, thus enabling clear career progression.

Methods of Study
There will be eight sessions over the academic year, usually on the second Thursday of each month from 9.30–4.00.

For whom the course is intended
Senior para-professional library staff working in or aspiring to first line management.

Entry requirements
It is expected that candidates will have City and Guilds 737, BTEC National Double Library Module, or equivalent.

Duration
The course runs from September to May.

Qualifications and methods of assessment
A college certificate will be awarded on completion of a written project at the end of the course Students will also be given the opportunity to be entered for NVQ level 3 for an extra fee. This requires some extra attendance at college.

Maximum numbers
Places on this course are limited to 15, and early application is advised.

Application and further details
Please contact Anne Totterdell, Library Education Tutor on 01823 366448.

Index